PAPA

WAS A PASTOR,

AND

MAMA

WAS A MINISTER

PRACTICAL DEMONSTRATIONS
OF THE FRUIT OF THE SPIRIT

NANCY MCDANIEL

ISBN 978-1-0980-6102-9 (paperback)
ISBN 978-1-0980-6103-6 (digital)

Christian Faith Publishing, Inc.
832 Park Avenue
Meadville, PA 16335
www.christianfaithpublishing.com

Printed in the United States of America

FROM GALATIANS 5:22

"Did I teach my little girl to lie?" The question hung in the air over the expectant congregation, like soaring swallows for what seemed like the longest time. The hard wood of the pews seemed to penetrate my little bottom as I squirmed and struggled in a futile effort to get comfortable under the scrutiny of so many pairs of eyes. There was no way to get comfortable as Papa was introducing the theme of his morning's sermon about the sinful nature of man. As often happened, he did not have to look very far to find his best sermon illustrations. There were always plenty of them to be found in the lives of his own family.

His topic that Sunday morning was the result of an ongoing theological discussion about original sin that he had been having for some time with a deacon who had a new baby. While looking with adoration at the perfect little toes and fingers, the man could not believe that this tiny perfect creature could be born bad. Papa continued his sermon solemnly, not ever quite focusing his gaze on the row of squirmy little girls.

He said, "We have to teach our little ones how to do everything: how to walk, talk, how to dress and eat. But when did you teach them to disobey and to lie? My daughter can look me directly in the eye when caught red-handed in the very act of disobedience and say, 'I did not do it, Papa!' How did she learn to tell a lie? Most parents, when their children reach the terrible twos, seem to accept the principle of original sin a little easier."

What a struggle we kids often had attempting to walk the thin line between honesty and rudeness. As PKs (preacher's kids), the congregation often held unrealistically high expectations for our behavior, and they were quick to confront our parents if we did not toe the proverbial line. Just a few Sundays later, I had been severely chastised for telling the wife of one of the deacons that she was too fat because she ate too much and was guilty of the terrible sin of gluttony. Even though this assessment was easily substantiated by following behind her in any line at the potluck dinners, I found out that honesty is not the best policy in every situation. Mama, the minister, would quietly teach us that "you don't have to tell everything you know or speak out every thought that goes through your head, ESPECIALLY if it is hurtful to someone else." The Apostle Paul had to write about that in many of his letters to the churches, reminding us that our speech should always be encouraging!

There are difficult decisions to make when you are a young child living in a congregational fishbowl. Our parents determined early on that, perhaps, the best way to learn life lessons was by example, rather than stern lecture or even "the board of education applied to the seat of learning." They constantly endeavored to demonstrate how to live our lives by allowing the Holy Spirit to guide our decisions and activities. Galatians 5:22 became a living example to us with every new day. Any time they missed the mark, they were quick to confess it to God and then to us. Throughout this book, I will try to give examples of every one of the Fruit of the Spirit and how it applies to family dynamics.

Chapter 1

THE FRUIT OF THE SPIRIT IS...
LOVE

Mama always was certain they theme dressed.
Patriotic outfits for July 4, 1976

All through our growing-up years, we learned the easy way (by observation) what the words in 1 Corinthians 13 actually meant by seeing our parents demonstrate the characteristics of love in their daily lives. We never had any doubts that their love was "to the moon and back." Even if we caught them in an occasional disagreement (usually over directions to a destination—this was before GPS), the conflict would always terminate with a quiet "I'm sorry, honey" and a hug and kiss. Every contact they had together brought an "I love you," and those three important little words were not rote or meaningless phrases but were always backed up with appropriate proof in their everyday caring actions. It was easily seen that Papa would do anything for his bride, and she reciprocated. The little phrase, "actions speak louder than words," was the real motto of our family life. Long before psychologists were expounding on the importance of touch and hugs every day for good psychological health, we reaped the benefit of our parent's consistent demonstrated actions of love.

This may sound like they were perfect, at least in our eyes, but they would be the first to share that they probably made their share of mistakes and poor decisions. As Papa frequently reminded us, kids did not come with an instruction manual. Since they were both the youngest child in their own families, they did not have the experience of caring for younger siblings. The difference may have been that they always covered every situation with proof that they loved us even though we were, sometimes (or often), naughty. For us, they "walked the talk" without many exceptions. The expectations for PKs were always over the unrealistically high for the members of the congregations. As we grew up, we saw other PKs grown to adulthood either falling closely in the footsteps of their parents by staying on the straight and narrow or, tragically for many, choosing the path of rebellion that left confusion and broken hearts behind. Our big sister, Judy, always said the rest of us were lucky because our parents practiced their parenting strategies on her, so it was easier for the rest of us down the line. There may have been a few rocky roads in the beginning, but they both learned from their overzealousness. How good it would be if we all could improve our parenting by simply not repeating mistakes.

One demonstration of romantic love that is very much a part of any pastor's family was the many weddings that happened in the congregation. These were always anticipated with great expectation and were very important events for all of us. Before Papa completed seminary and became a pastor, our parents' usual function in wedding ceremonies was to be vocalists singing beautiful love songs or to give brides away in the absence of family (especially during the war years) or, sometimes, to be the essential witnesses. The first wedding that we have pictorial memories of occurred when I was two years old and selected to be the flower girl for the wedding of one of the navy men in our church. There were many rehearsals at home to teach the fine points of petal dropping down the aisle. It took quite a while that day to get the beautiful long dress just right and the always unruly curls in some sort of order. In the rush of getting everyone ready, no one remembered little girls need to go potty, especially when very excited. The bridal music started, the lovely bridesmaids, in their rainbow of colored dresses, paraded down the aisle, and the flower girl followed them, carefully dropping the petals all the way down the aisle. However, once I arrived at the required position up front, nature called urgently. I started tugging on the maid of honor's hand, saying in a loud voice, "I have to go potty," but she just held on tighter to prevent a runaway disruption of the sacred moments. The little voice got louder and more demanding with each passing moment. Papa and Mama were in the choir loft singing and could not intervene. They watched helplessly as the squirms and protests became more pronounced. The pastor, in desperation to continue the ceremony, said, "Please let her go before there is an accident." The wedding guests watched in amazement as the little flower girl started back up the aisle, resolutely dropping the remaining petals all the way to the exit door. My relieved parents intercepted the procession and insured the ladies' room was the next stop.

As I reached teenage years and listened again to Mama sharing that very funny story with a bride-to-be planning her own special day, Mama confessed to us that she had tears in her eyes during that entire experience. Not tears of embarrassment but from the knowledge that before she knew it, she would witness her own child walking down another bridal aisle in her own long white wedding gown. Time really flies for parents, a lesson that I, too, would discover in the not too distant future.

A spin-off from that wedding occurred later in 1944, while we were still living in San Diego during World War II. The wedding photographer was challenged to get a picture for the paper to remind the subscribers to support the troops fighting so diligently for our freedom. He remembered the little flower girl with unruly curls and thought that child would be perfect for the front page article. He wanted the emphasis to be the importance of children praying for the soldiers in battle. To graphically illustrate his point, he placed me in front of a lighted candelabra and told me to pray. That was an easy request for a preacher's kid. Dutifully, I recited the little prayer we were all taught as soon as we could speak. "We bow our head, fold our hands, and close our eyes when we pray, to keep our mind and thoughts upon the words we say." The pictures were taken, and he seemed very happy with the results. The next Sunday morning, when the paper was delivered to our front door, the praying child's picture was printed with a scene of soldiers fighting in battle superimposed over the top. My reaction was not surprise that my picture was in the paper but rather, a scientific concern: "How them guys get fightin' in the sky?"

The picture they used in the San Diego newspaper with caption "our children pray for our soldiers"—it was December 1944.

Papa always felt that weddings were a wonderful part of his ministry. After all, the scripture uses marriage as an example of the special intimate relationship that Christ has with His church.

He felt a huge obligation to ensure that the couple wanting to be married had adequate preparation and the counseling necessary to make this a true commitment. He was delighted that his batting average was above normal for the couples entrusted to his care as a representative of God and the state of California. He developed a special habit of always giving back to the bride whatever gift the groom gave him for conducting the service. He would hand the unopened envelope to the bride and say, "Use this for your honeymoon. It is what your new husband thinks you are worth." One groom was justifiably mortified when his bride opened the envelope and a dollar bill fell out, but most of the time, the couples were very grateful for the unexpected donation for their honeymoon. Papa always felt that the kids in his church were an extension of our family, and his delight in being able to participate in their marriage service was evident to all.

As we think back over the years, some weddings we attended were very fancy, others very plain, but all were very memorable. Papa said, after conducting hundreds of weddings, that he had never seen an ugly bride. No matter what they looked like the day before, they were all radiant and lovely for their special moment. Papa loved to remind us of a very sophisticated black tail wedding that took place at the Wee Kirk o' the Heather chapel at Forest Lawn Cemetery. (As kids, we had a tough time understanding why someone would want to get married in a cemetery—does that mean they were dying for the opportunity to be together?) The carefully manicured lawn had automatic sprinklers that had thoroughly wet the grass between the men's dressing area and the chapel. The groom, who was running a little late (due to uncooperative cuff links and studs), suddenly was aware that he heard the appropriate entry music, so he left the meandering sidewalk and took a wild shortcut across the lawn. Too late, he realized that the wet grass would make his pant legs very wet, so he reached down and rolled them up to his knee. Upon reaching the chapel door, the magnitude of the moment surpassed all practicalities, and he forgot to unroll his pants. The wedding pictures were hilarious. Many guests tried to subtly get the message across, but all their attempts failed. The entire wedding was conducted with the groom in knee-high pants and black tails. It was a true California informal/formal wedding.

Another groom in a wedding at the beautiful colonial-looking First Baptist Church of Hollywood was very anxious and worried that everything would go just perfectly. The wedding had been planned to the last detail to reflect his bride's childhood dreams. Every part was carried out to exquisite perfection, until the couple knelt at the altar for the prayer of consecration. The beautiful notes of "The Lord's Prayer" introduction started but were disturbed by the noises of nervous giggling from the audience. The groomsmen had perversely painted, in bright red letters, "HELP ME" on the soles of the groom's brand-new patent leather shoes. There was some very righteous indignation expressed over the prank, but those attending never forgot that ceremony or the day that couple stated their vows of love.

Another nervous bride, gorgeous in her lovely gown with a humungous hooped skirt, was waiting near the door for the last bridesmaid to make an entrance. Her father was whispering last-minute words of encouragement and wisdom when, suddenly, a neighborhood cat came around the corner stalking a bird. It was startled by the unexpected people and darted under the relative safety of the large hoop skirt. As the bride shrieked, the cat frantically ran around and around trying to escape. It took quite a while to get the wedding back on track without the extra uninvited feline guest and to calm the hysterical bride. The poor organist had played the bridal march over and over without any sign of the bride for over ten minutes. However, soon, the familiar words were spoken, "Dearly beloved, we are gathered together in the sight of God and these witnesses," and the wedding commenced without further incidents.

*****

As we girls grew up and were witnesses of many couples tying the knot, we were able to begin to see what went right and what went really wrong. It was then that many of our own dreams were made about the wedding we would have someday. Growing up with an all-girl house was so much fun. We were able to participate in and witness many types of weddings. We saw firsthand when huge layered cakes started to slip when the icing melted in the heat of the outside reception, groomsmen, who fell like telephone poles during the rigid ceremonies, and little flower girls, who panicked with all of the people looking at them and ran for their mommies, or ring bearers who could not part with the pillow for the ring ceremony. Planning our own weddings became a pretty easy task, for once forewarned was forearmed.

Our own weddings were memorable for many reasons. We wanted to be married in Lakeview Chapel at Hume Lake Christian Conference Grounds. It is a very special part of both of our spiritual walks. My husband was part of the first camp in the '40s when they slept in tents by the creek. I spent most summers there as a child while we built our cabin and, later, worked on the summer staff in high school and first years of college. Plus, my love proposed after a hike to Little Brown Church by Inspiration Point. Somehow, permission was granted to have the service at 4:00 p.m. on a Sunday afternoon of Labor Day weekend. (Most of our guests were from at least one to four hours travel time away.) A dilemma we encountered was that I wanted Papa to give me away, but we both also wanted him to marry us. That problem was solved by having a special friend, Kenny Poure, a wonderful youth evangelist, to be in charge of the first part of the service and then Papa took over after "Who giveth this woman to be married to this man? Her mother and I" and then he took his place at the front. In his excitement, he forgot his little black book that had the traditional wedding ceremony printed in it. To make matters worse, we had memorized our vows, which also threw him off a bit. The usual ceremony order was further mixed when, unexpectedly, the groom started singing to his bride, "I'll be loving you, Always." Poor Papa wasn't sure what was coming next. Then of course, there was the unexpected emotion of this bride being his own firstborn daughter. With tears in his eyes, we do not think he could have read the familiar words anyway. To this day, my husband wonders if we are really married because Papa forgot several parts of the service including the "I now pronounce you man and wife." Are we really married? I truly hope so, after two sons and fifty-eight years together.

Little sister Linda followed our example to be married at Hume Lake the following summer. Her wedding almost was postponed for she had a very serious car accident on the way to work from Biola twenty-five days before her wedding that left her partially scalped. Thankfully, the laceration was mostly from just below her hairline but required shaving the top of her head and repairing laceration with 350 stitches. Mama, in her true creative form, helped Linda find a wig that looked very much like her hair. The wedding pictures verify that, unless you knew the story, you would not be able to tell the hair wasn't still secured to her head. She named the wig Greta and has it to this day as a reminder of a very close call. As another example of Christian love, all her professors at Biola waived her finals and gave her the grades she had going into those last weeks. Papa always claimed that during the ceremony at the vows, that he said "Will you, Paul, take Greta to be your wedded wig?" (Just like our Papa to remember it that way).

One of the foundational requirements Papa had when he was asked by couples to marry them was several sessions of joint premarital counseling. He had learned that many of the pitfalls that cause marriages to break up could be avoided with simple discussions before the fact. So unless a couple agreed to this, he would suggest they find another person to conduct their service. Over the years, his record was amazing. A very high percentage of marriages were successful over the long term, especially those who listened to the Scripture's advice in Ecclesiastes 4:12, "A cord of three strands are not easily broken." This verse became one of our life verses. As we faced many daunting challenges of life, like breast cancer and pancreatic and kidney failure, that third strand kept us tightly together. Papa also practiced what he preached about marriage. He always told us that while he was the head of the house, Mama was the neck! Even though she was a very young girl when he married her, only seventeen years, she had a maturity way beyond her years that would help her through the many difficult parts of their ministry. She exemplified the Fruit of the Spirit, and her gentle tone and touch could defuse the most explosive situations.

While growing up, we always asked for the stories about their own romance. The young nineteen-year-old choir director that came to the very little church in East Los Angeles to fulfill his required outreach duties from Biola College immediately saw a lovely eleven-year-old in the choir that sang like an angel. Papa was smitten but knew he had to go to school, and she had to grow up. With the expenses of school, Papa could not afford the trolley fare of ten cents to get to his twice-weekly commitment for choir practice and Sunday services, so he walked more than six miles from the campus in downtown Los Angeles to the little church in East LA each Wednesday and Sunday. After he finally proved his worth to the small congregation, they awarded him his first salary in the ministry—twenty cents a week for the trolley car fare.

Papa said that he knew immediately that this girl that sang like an angel was THE ONE! However, getting married was not possible with the responsibilities of life in the way, plus she was carefully guarded by her father, brother, and two brothers-in-law. So he cultivated a wonderful friendship and enjoyed their mutual love of music. He dated other people and waited for time to pass. Until Mama was about fourteen and a half years, she had little use for this tall, dark, and handsome man that all the girls in the church swooned over. During this hiatus, Papa was taking vocal lessons from Madame Blanc, an opera star from Germany. He used good tactics in his pursuit of Mama by arranging for her to have vocal lessons after school with the famous teacher too. While studying an operatic aria about love, Madame Blanc suggested Mama think about Leland to project the necessary emotion in the song. Mama responded, "I don't think what I feel about him is what you are looking for in this." It had not yet sunk in that Papa was winning in his pursuit. He came frequently to check on Mama's vocal progress, even after he was sent to other assignments and did not have the satisfaction of regular contacts.

For 2 years he traveled with Biola quartet in concert

Grandpa finally allowed some "courting" to occur when Mama had her fifteenth birthday. Most of the time, that meant family dinners, church services, or group outings. However, one night after supper, at their home the month before she was sixteen years old, Papa bravely pulled her into the living room and onto his lap. Hiding behind the evening paper from curious family members, he took three rings from his pocket and casually asked, "Which one do you want?" He never officially asked her to marry him, but convinced her that it was essential to be engaged. He thought that fact would protect him from the girls at college that chased him from event to event as well as being good insurance for keeping the other guys away from his angel. Mama chose the largest of the three rings, which cost all of thirty-five dollars, a huge sum in the day. It is a reflection of his character that the jeweler allowed him to have all three rings from the store without even a deposit.

Some of Papa's old girlfriends became family legends. One that we kids especially loved to hear about was Fermalline Cassebeer (we always naturally called her Firmline Case of Beer). Sometimes, we did not know how much was real and how much he made up to just entertain us. We were all familiar with photos of his early dashing days, so we knew that he could live up to his romantic reputation. When he was first going to Los Angeles Junior College, he sang in a chorus with the daughter of Mr. Lockheed. The Lockheed family lived in a mansion on the top of Mulhulland Drive overlooking the city. Papa's old Model T car could hardly make it up there to pick her up for the special rehearsals and concerts. Many dashing potential playboy suitors in their fancy sports cars stood in awe as she came running out and cheerfully jumped in the old Model T. How could he dare to rub shoulders with the rich and famous? His motto was confidence! He felt that a person could get in any door if you acted like you belonged.

Our parents got married on June 11, 1939, only nine days before Mama graduated from high school. It was quite an event. They had to use the Montebello Methodist Church rather than Mama's tiny home church because it held 300 plus people. Were they all surprised when more than 500 people showed up for the wedding! Many well-wishers had to be content watching the celebration through the open sanctuary window.

Because Papa had always been such a prankster, there were many sinister plots afloat to add unplanned excitement to their wedding. He had an additional very necessary (make money) job in the mail room of the *Los Angeles Times*. This is where the parts of the paper are stuffed together after printing. Later, we laughed at thinking God had given him that experience in preparation for all the bulletins that had to be printed and assembled in future churches. The very rough guys that worked with him at the paper planned to shanghai him after work the night before the wedding and drive him to the desert where he would be abandoned. They had bets on what kind of ingenuity he would use to get back to the city by the next afternoon. Thankfully for Mama and the wedding plans, his sympathetic boss overheard the plot and told him "Fuzzy, you better get out of here quick." He was able to leave work early by a little-used back door and avoid the planned kidnapping. Another plot was hatched by his older brother, Uncle Punky, who had been the brunt of many of Papa's practical jokes as they grew up. Uncle Punky planned to chain him to a telephone pole. That prank was derailed by his own wife's vigilance! Her sense of propriety would not allow him to jeopardize their special day.

The actual wedding proceeded on time as planned with all the participants and was beautiful of course. Mama had enlisted the help of her six girlfriends from school who were joined by six church friends to sing many of their concert love songs as a ladies' ensemble. Mama led them skillfully from the doorway. The church organist had just purchased a new instrument called a vibraharp. She learned to play it just in time as a special treat. As always during their life special moments, music was the focal point of their blessed events. As was common in that day, many people had planned to chivaree them after the reception and had many other plans to cause havoc, but a friend of Papa's, in his new Lincoln Zephyr (the hot car of the day), came zooming up and whisked them away before anyone could get to their cars to follow and disturb the honeymoon.

A real painful occurrence happened to destroy photographic memories, when a young child tripped over the tripod legs, bringing the camera crashing down to the ground and exposing all the used film. The only picture they had of their wedding was a snapshot taken in their friend's backyard just before they changed from their wedding outfits to honeymoon clothes. This picture was a cherished treasure of our parents over the years. It always had a place of honor in their bedrooms. As a wonderful surprise, my younger sister Linda had it sketched by a Bay Area artist for their fiftieth wedding anniversary. Linda now has that special picture in her home to always remember our parents and their wonderful wedding day.

After a very brief get-acquainted honeymoon, Mama had to return to her childhood home to finish high school, while her new husband journeyed to Salinas for his first full-time job as music and youth director. This summer job gave him the understanding of what the ministry was really about. The pastor of the church was building his dream house in Carmel in preparation for retirement and only came back to town to preach the sermon on Sundays. Papa had to do everything else during the week to hold the congregation together. He quickly learned about crisis intervention, counseling and encouraging the sick, visitation of the dying and consoling grieving families as well as trying to bring hope and comfort at the resulting funerals. It was a joy to him when his beloved was able to officially come to his side as his helpmate.

Finances were always a problem in the ministry. The starting salary was $100 per month, and that required careful budgeting. They had a car payment of $35 a month, $15 for apartment rental, and they put aside $35 for expenses of hauling the church kids around to sings and activities every week. This did not leave much for food and other essentials, but somehow, like Elijah's pot of oil, the essential payments were always there by God's provision.

Mama's unforgettable fox fur collar

During their brief time in Salinas, a wealthy elderly woman in the church took an interest in Mama, who reminded her of her own beloved granddaughter who had recently passed away. She plied Mama with gifts, including a lovely hope chest that she treasured all her life, and a very expensive suit with a real fox fur collar, including its head and tiny feet. She wore it for special occasions when we were little. My sister was intrigued and liked to pet it, especially during church when we had to be quiet. I was terrified it was going to bite me and could not even sit close to her. This fur collar is a vivid memory for both of us to this day. When the summer assignment was over, the lady really wanted our parents to stay there, but the church budget would not allow it with the new pastor. She even volunteered to pay his salary. This idea was soundly rejected by Papa, who strongly felt that only the church itself should assume fiscal responsibility for the staff.

Even after our parents left Salinas to return to Los Angeles, the special lady kept in close contact with them. When she heard the news that they were expecting their first child, she sent them a complete layette. She realized how difficult finances could be in the ministry, and she didn't want the little one to lack any essentials upon arrival.

Papa reuniting with one of those Shuler boys now an evangelist

The folks returned to Trinity Methodist Church in Los Angeles, where Papa worked as youth director for Dr. "Fighting Bob" Shuler. This man of God felt compelled to take on all the corruption in the City of Angels. Many times, the LAPD had to place barricades around the church to control the crowds who came to watch, but his fiery sermons were very effective in reaching lost people. When we were little girls, Papa often entertained us with tales of the Shuler PKs. The boys often felt the need to assist their father in presenting his sermons with more realism. The congregation never knew quite what to expect from their shenanigans. Once, during a real hellfire-and-brimstone sermon, the worshipers were disturbed by the smell of sulfur and smoke coming through the wall cracks and heater vents. In real panic, they got up and ran from the church shouting, "FIRE!" The service was totally disrupted, the boys were caught in the act and soundly disciplined by their father, although Papa always thought he was secretly proud of their endeavors to provide realistic illustrations for his sermons.

The first picture of their first born. Mama was about 6 months pregnant in front of their "Honeymoon House" that Papa built with help from his grandfather

Papa had been taught by his parents that land ownership was important for fiscal security, so in the entire time of his ministry, they only lived in an actual church parsonage two times—the first in Buttonwillow and then in Hanford. His start-up money came from savings from many extra jobs while he was in college. The newlyweds' first little honeymoon house, Papa built with his own hands, with the help of his maternal grandfather, Grandpa Newton, who was a skilled carpenter. Mama even got to help a little bit with the roofing. Papa always pointed with pride to the crooked row of shingles that his bride had nailed. As became his pattern for houses in the future, he had no architectural drawings or plans. The house just grew like "topsy" under his skillful determination and hard work. The little house may have had only bare essentials, but it was home and the beginning of a family legacy.

Mama knew early on that this charming man had a very tender heart, especially for little children. He was very ahead of his time in participating in infant care. When they had their first baby girl just a month after the bombing of Pearl Harbor, they understood that their baby could not interfere with all the activities he had as church youth director and administrator of the care for the military. So with her usual flexibility and resourcefulness, Mama made an extra-long carrying basket that would allow them to care for the baby and manage all the travel required too (this was before infant car seats or portable beds). One Sunday afternoon, they were going to grab a quick bite of lunch before having to meet the church's softball team. Papa was in charge of the baby while Mama was eating. True to form, I was wiggling and wiggling! Papa was at a loss until he felt something warm going down his leg. As he looked down in trepidation, he saw what looked like his leg covered in chocolate pudding, but the smell verified the awful truth! He had to race back to church for a quick cleanup and overhaul before he heard that important first inning "Batters up" call, and the ballgame began.

Papa always got up with us at night when we were fussy because he knew that Mama needed rest to handle the difficulties of the day. However, even after feeding me one night, the initial successful remedy, I continued to fuss, so Papa placed me in the carrying basket and put it on his tummy. He was hoping the gentle rocking motion would soothe the cries. He then promptly fell asleep, with the basket teeter tottering on top of his lap. It was not long into his sleep that he heard a crash and a scream as basket, baby, and all fell to the floor. The screaming sounded like serious injury, but thankfully, little ones are made of hard stuff, and the only damage was Mama's jangled nerves.

Even when we girls were older (three years and five years) and developed rheumatic fever, with its tremendously painful joint aches, most hurting nights, we can remember Papa picking us up and rocking us in the big chair while rubbing the aching parts and singing a gentle soothing melody. Somehow, those ministering moments helped the pain more than the aspirin or other remedies prescribed by our physician. The love they showed us even helped with the painful blood tests that had to be endured each week. It has never ceased to amaze me how the warm hugs of a loving parent can soothe away pain and its memories. At the difficult doctor visits, they usually found an ice cream stand or a little toy to make the visit less unpleasant in our memories. How they ever managed two little girls in bed for two years is beyond me, but bed rest was the only known treatment in those days. So enduring all of the uncomfortable moments was a necessity.

As a parent now, I can really sympathize with their fear and frustration as they anxiously did everything possible to help their little ones get better. They spent many evenings, as we fitfully slept, beseeching their Heavenly Father to intercede. How they managed to keep their little ones entertained for the many months confined to bed is hard to imagine, but their love was the essential ingredient that brought us through the difficult times.

Often, we were reminded by word and deed that there are three kinds of love: *friendship* (phileo), *romantic* (eros), and *agape*—God's unconditional love. All three are needed during our relationships on earth. In their lives, Papa and Mama gave living examples of all these types of love. Friends knew they could always count on their help, support, encouragement, and understanding. Their door was always open for any need. They also demonstrated the huge commitment to their wedding vows and exemplified the real love that honors your mate. "For better or for worse, for richer or poorer, in sickness and in health, to love and to cherish until death do us part!"

Their lives demonstrated that love is not just how you feel, but it is something that you do—an act of your will. Even more important, they had as a goal that their lives would always reflect the *love* of God.

Chapter 2

THE FRUIT
OF THE SPIRIT IS LOVE...
JOY

Music was a thread of joy throughout our lives growing up. Some of our favorite early songs were, "I have the joy, joy, joy, joy down in my heart." (We added up in my head, down in my feet, and all over me. I am sure the author would not object to his words being added to.) Another song we often sang was "Jesus and others and you, what a wonderful way to spell JOY." This song got us through all our everyday chores. Our folks always used it in Sunday school, where they would loudly lead with the special posters of JOY that Mama created for selected children to hold up during the song. Usually, all of them put on their best behavior so they would be the fortunate ones chosen to lead.

> Jesus and others and you, what a wonder-
> ful way to spell JOY
> Jesus and others and you, in the life of
> each girl and each boy
> J is for Jesus for He has first place
> O is for others we meet face-to-face
> Y is for you in whatever you do
> Put yourself last and spell JOY
> (author unknown, I have never seen it in
> printed music)

This important message was molded early into our hearts so that, as we grew up and pursued service-type positions, meeting the needs of others took its proper place after putting Jesus first.

Whether we were doing disagreeable chores, like housecleaning or being cooped up in the car for long distances, singing became our coping mechanism. Everyone in the family was expected to help with chores, and our rotating list was posted. Many times, we would sulk and want to play outside with the neighbor kids, and our parents would burst into "If you're happy and you know it clap your hands" or "I'm so happy here's the reason why, Jesus took my burdens all away." Our parents knew it was very hard to be grumpy and disagreeable while singing songs about joy.

Papa and Mama sang at many fund raisers and youth meetings. This one was at a mansion on Mulhulland Drive in Hollywood Hills

We learned most of our early Bible verses and the books of the Bible by song. Even after many decades, when the pastor says to turn to a little-utilized book like one of the minor prophets, I find myself having to sing the verse of the song to locate the appropriate spot in the Bible. It is peculiar that I can still remember all the verses of those childhood songs, and each time I recall the words, they still invoke a sense of joy, bring a smile, and ease troubled thoughts or anxiety.

We, kids, learned our first anatomy lesson from Ezekiel as Papa taught us the old spiritual melody "Now Hear the Word of the Lord." The head bone connected to the neck bone, the neck bone connected to the shoulder bone, the shoulder bone connected to the back bone, etc. In college years, when I was struggling with the complexities of anatomy and trying to remember all the bone names and positions, remembering this little song brought a smile. On long trips in the car, we learned many songs and how to harmonize! Papa sang bass, Mama sang tenor, I sang alto, and my little sister a clear soprano. Sometimes, they would switch the parts around to give us the opportunity to hear how it would be to sing other parts. By the time we were in school, we regularly sang special trios at the Rescue Mission, for funerals, church meetings, etc. It was a wonderful preparation for auditioning for school choirs. Sacred music was not the only music we were exposed to, although it was always given preeminence. We learned early on to appreciate classical music, folk songs, and popular music.

When I was just four years old, Papa's friend from Biola College needed a child to sing a song to be used for the mission field. Papa arranged for the recording after teaching me the simple melody:

> I do believe, I now believe that Jesus died for me,
> And through His blood, His precious blood,
> I am now from sin set free!

At that time, this gospel message in a nutshell sung by a little child was felt to be an important evangelistic tool and used all over Africa, India, and China by missionary friends.

Papa and Mama were called upon frequently to lead worship or do special music for Christian Endeavor events, many weddings, funerals, banquets, etc. One of their favorite songs was "Indian Love Call." They sang it often for churches' Valentine banquets or adult parties, and we knew all the words before we could read. Another fun favorite of theirs was frequently requested at church sings.

Mama would sing, "What's your name little boy?"

Papa replied, "My name in Lemmy."

"Lemmy what, little boy?"

"Lemmy kiss you! What's your name, little girl?"

"My name is Ida."

"Ida what, little girl?"

"I don't want to!"

The second verse accelerated, "What's your name little girl, My name is Laska, Laska what little girl, Laska my Mommy." And finally, "What's your name little girl, My name is Aly, Aly what little girl, Aly right!" The little song always ended in a big kiss. We and the many audiences never tired of this little song, maybe because of the great JOY that was evident when they sang it.

Sometimes, learning songs by repetition before we could read created problems for us. I still remember puzzling over why we sang about Gladys the cross-eyed bear (Gladly the cross I'll bear). Another puzzle was why we sang "Bringing in the She's" (Bringing in the Sheaves). I was very worried until it was clarified that there was something really wrong when only the girls had to be brought into Heaven. We had lengthy discussions with other little friends who thought the same song said "bringing in the sheep." Other times, we added words to the music that seemed to make sense for us such as: "when the roll is called up yonder pass the butter." Some of the more pious deacons had difficulty with these lyrics and would complain bitterly to our parents about our "cutting up and lack of respect for sacred things." Somehow, they would leave the discussions less upset and certain that we would be dealt with in short order, but rarely did we get scolded for our embellishments.

Another one of Mamas' special ministry gifts was her creativity with flowers. Our yards were always full of flowers that she utilized to bring joy to many people. Each Mother's Day, she would make lovely corsages to be awarded to special mothers during the worship service. The oldest mother present, the youngest mother, the one with the most children, the one that travelled the furthest, etc. These special tributes brought much joy to many of the church ladies each year. Mama also made certain that there were flowers in front of the pulpit each Sunday and then she recycled the arrangements into little bouquets to take to the sick or shut-in during the week. She was very creative in making the bouquets, and we always thought, without any bias, that her arrangements looked nicer than those supplied by local florists because they were made with lots of love.

Like most pastors' wives of the time, Mama was expected to fill in the gaps and cover all bases. She was expected to play the piano if there was no one in the congregation responsible for that job. Without having any formal piano lessons, she played most of the music by ear and could figure out quickly most hymn tunes with basic chords. However, she longed to play classical music or more difficult sacred transcriptions by reading the notes. To prevent this problem with her girls, somehow, she found money in the limited budget to pay for thirty-minute piano lessons. The piano teacher let us start as soon as we could sit still on the bench. The teacher was an elderly lady who always had a stern countenance, and we were scared to death of her. She was the one who vividly taught us the difficult difference between the words "can and may." If our anxiety caused a need to use the bathroom, and we said "Can I go to the bathroom," she would say "NO! You probably can go to the bathroom, but you may NOT." Looking back, I am surprised she didn't get a wet piano bench.

Infamous piano recital note the oxford saddle shoes (NO Mary Janes)

Like most kids, we hated the daily piano practice required (especially when we could hear the neighborhood kids outdoors playing baseball in the alley), but we loved the JOY of performing. Our teacher's piano recitals were always formal dress. So the yearly event, where prizes were awarded after the students completed their painful attempts at the required musical selection, meant a lovely new long dress and black patent leather shoes (Mary Janes). As the recital picture demonstrated, the folks did not have enough funds that month to cover new shoes, so the front row had a few pair of oxford saddle shoes. New outfits made the stress of having to perform in front of a crowd of people without errors usually worth it. As we developed a grow- ing ability to play piano, we were soon also put to work at the church playing for young people's meetings or primary Sunday school classes. The very little preschoolers were the easiest to play for since they did not complain about wrong notes as we tried to play the little songs like "Climb, Climb Up Sunshine Mountain" or "This Little Light of Mine."

From the beginning, when Papa pastored his first church in Buttonwillow, he always incorporated a time in the worship service especially for the children. Sometimes, he did a children's message using magic or chemical object lessons, but later, Mama took that on as her own ministry, leaving Papa more time for his sermon preparation. She developed elaborate flannel graph boards, which graphically demonstrated her creativity. She would spend hours painting amazing backgrounds that showed the Bible story times or the necessary backdrops for the stories. Our favorite was the Ipsi and Newman series. We learned to make appropriate decisions in moral dilemmas by watching what happened to their struggles. Ipsi was an ugly man representing our sin nature that lived in our "heart house" and was always doing battle with Newman, the strong clean-cut athlete who represented our new good life in Christ. When the child in a story did the right thing, Newman was the victor and grew stronger, taking a larger part of the heart house. However, if the child made wrong choices, Newman was pushed into a corner, and the ugly Ipsi was victorious. Even though we heard these stories many times through the years, we never tired of them for they reinforced the importance of making right decisions and the consequences suffered when wrong choices were made.

Stories of the life of Jesus and His miracles were always a foundational part of the flannel graph stories. One year, Papa and Mama carefully constructed a lovely garden scene, with the tomb built into it. It was a three-dimensional background, with a stone that rolled away. They utilized it for the first time on Easter Sunday to demonstrate the power of the Resurrection. The back of the board had a little box built into it for the actual tomb. All the little children would listen in awe as Mama placed the doll representing the carefully wrapped body of the crucified Savior into the tomb. The Roman soldiers would then roll the stone in front of the tomb, with the guards placed nearby. The story continued with early that morning, the women came to find the stone rolled away and the angel sitting on the top asking, "Why seek ye the living among the dead?" We would then hold our collective breaths as a very excited child chosen from the audience came to check the tomb. They would put in their little hand and pull out only an empty shell of grave clothes demonstrating "He Is Risen"! Year after year, that story was retold, and little children were so excited when they found the body was gone. It was a real miracle right in front of our very eyes.

It was not for many years later that, in exploring the set, we found that Mama had placed the little body representing the crucified Jesus under the stone ledge that had a little folded cloth hanging over the edge to hide it. Her very creative way of demonstrating a miracle changed many lives. As they closed their last home after retiring from full-time ministry, we girls cleaned out the accumulation of years of study and teaching stored in their garage. It was a tearful moment for all of us when we found the tattered and torn flannel graph board with the story of the Resurrection and realized it would no longer bring wonder and *joy* to other little children at Easter worship service. Easter was always a joyful event for us girls because we each got a new Sunday dress and new shoes. While still living in Los Angeles, we were awakened very early at 4:00 a.m. to dress and travel to the Rose Bowl, where many of the area churches combined for an amazing sunrise service. Papa usually led the music, which was an additional thrill as the sun peaked over the Horizon while Mama held on to two very sleepy little girls.

In our family, it was agreed that the *joy* of Christmas was the highlight of the year. Papa went over and above trying to make it a special time for his girls. He would stop on Christmas Eve, after we had gone to bed, and buy a beautiful Charlie Brown-type Christmas tree. Often, it was the only one left, and the owner would just give it to him so the lot could close and the staff go home. Then he would stay up half the night trimming it with Mama's special antique ornaments and the popcorn strings we made so Christmas day would be super special for his girls. He also filled our stockings with fruit and nuts. Sometimes, there was a little leftover cash to put in a small toy. We each got our hearts' desire gift. My little sister always wanted storybook dolls, while I favored an old fashioned baby doll with wooden carved head and a durable cloth body called Susie Q. Subsequent Christmas celebrations brought more items for the dolls wardrobe and playhouse fixtures.

Our birthdays were the second most *joyful* day of the year. In some ways, we felt selfishly it was the most joyful since it was not shared with anyone else. Although resources were limited, our parents always found a way to make each birthday very special. Practical needs were met, with one of the presents always being much-needed underwear and socks. A special delight when we were little girls was a plastic container that held the magical week of panties: each one was a different color with the day written in script. Now we wonder if that was Mamas attempt to be sure that we changed them regularly. On Saturday morning, the family wash day, it was easy to count how many were there.

The birthday person always got their choice of menu for the evening meal. Mama would carefully include our favorite cake; mine was the miracle of Baked Alaska. We never could understand how the angel food cake filled with frozen ice cream could survive the heat of a hot oven while the covering layer of meringue browned. My own birthday menu never wavered while I was growing up. The only meat I would eat as a child was hot dogs, so my menu was grilled hot dogs stuffed with American Cheese, cooked spinach, and cooked carrots with store-bought rolls and strawberry jam. You can only imagine what JOY that menu brought to the family, but at least, they only had to eat it once a year!

Most Saturday mornings were a source of joy for our family because everyone was usually home from work. Papa, who worked every day twenty out of twenty-four hours, always made it a priority to be home for family Saturday mornings. Even while still in seminary with all its demands, working part time as a youth director at the church, and supplementing his meager income by working the night shift Friday and Saturday nights at the *Times* newspaper, he would appear fresh as a daisy for our family time. Mama would add to the specialness of the day by making pancakes. She would create bunnies, bears, snowpeople, and all sorts of shapes to thrill our hearts. After breakfast, everyone would help out to get the washing done, the house cleaned, and all chores completed so we could have a family adventure. Sometimes, it was a bike ride or a hike through the park, a trip to the zoo, a ride to the beach to jump the waves and make sand castles or a trip to the nearby mountains or, our personal favorite, ice skating with the neighborhood kids at the Polar Palace. California had so many things to explore and to see; we never could really do it all, but we certainly tried. While Papa was still in seminary, our outings were sometimes camouflaged as exploring the campus, giving him the opportunity to slip away to the library to do necessary research for his assignments. No matter what it was, we were always together, and that made us full of JOY.

Our animals were another source of joy for our family. One of the first dogs we remember hearing about was Bimbo, a little Boston bull terrier. Our parents had gotten him during one of their earliest jobs in Ventura at St John's Methodist Church. (Recently, while exploring the area, we found that the little church was still there, but it had been preserved as a historical monument and converted to a wedding chapel.) Bimbo proudly watched our parents bring home their first baby girl. Although he was a very small dog, he was very protective, and Mama could put me safely out on the front lawn on a blanket for him to watch. He had a good herding instinct, and with the natural development, rolling over crawling, etc., he would gently push me back on the blanket. Many of those passing by would stop to watch, but he would not allow anyone in the yard. For my first birthday, Mama spent much of the morning making her first from-scratch cake. However, that afternoon, Papa's brother and family came to celebrate and brought a magnificent store-bought cake. Rather than use both, Mama put her cake aside on the drainboard to use the next day with the church family. However, when they returned from church with friends to continue the celebration, they found a guilty-looking Bimbo with cake crumbs all over his face and only a tiny piece left on the plate. The poor dog was in the "dog house" for sure, but he never tried to eat cake again. He went with us to Papa's new job during the war in San Diego, where they found out they were expecting a little sister, so Bimbo's babysitting job would be doubled. However, one day, while they were walking on the beach with Bimbo, a navy patrol convinced them to give up their precious dog for the sake of the war effort. We never heard how they used him, but the whole family was proud of their contribution of their very own "War Dog."

We kids did not really remember any other significant pets until we were in school. Our parents used their meager savings to purchase a little house at 1224 N Hobart in Hollywood, only a few miles from where Papa's new position at South Hollywood Presbyterian Church was located. The house had a very small yard because it also had a tiny bungalow on the back of the property and a very small apartment on the side of the house. They could rent these out to help with the mortgage payments. That house was not good for having a dog, since there was no fenced-in area, so we had to be content with fish, frogs, and cats. Papa also finally got to have his lifelong desire for a large aquarium of tropical fish. They were always so soothing to watch. There were angel fish, beautiful neon fish, the very prolific guppies, and a strange fish called a Dojo that lived on the bottom of the sand. Sometimes all you could see was his eyes sticking out above the grains of sand! Whenever Papa had the task of cleaning out the tank, we girls and half the neighborhood kids would line up to watch him catch all the fish with a little net. One time, in his haste to complete the work, he missed seeing the Dojo hiding in the sand at the bottom. All the fish were transferred to another container, and he began the cleaning job. As he moved the suction tube across the bottom, sucking up the waste and debris, there was a sudden thump, and the children all gasped in horror as the Dojo was caught in the tube. Although successfully rescued still alive after his ordeal, the accident seemed to bend him over, and for the rest of his life, he looked like a question mark. Even after all the trauma he endured, he lived in seeming contentment at the bottom of the tank for many years following the incident. He was never sucked up again because his little bend was out of the sand and easy to see.

Papa's aquarium also gave us an early introduction to the problems of nature. The mama guppies seemed to get pregnant all the time, and if Papa did not catch the mamas in time to put them in another container for delivery, all the baby fish would be eaten by the other fish in moments. Papa would watch carefully and put the pregnant guppies in their own little private mason jar until the babies grew big enough to put all of them back in the big tank.

Our animal graveyard in the back was very full by the time we moved away from the Hollywood house, since many of our pets had shortened life spans due to the hazards of the city. We lost many cats that would sneak out of the house with an open door and were hit by cars as they tried to negotiate the alley or street. Some of Papa's fish seemed to have a very short life span, and we would find them in the morning belly up, floating at the top of the tank. All of these were awarded special funerals, with little coffins out of matchboxes or shoe boxes lined with a scrap of satiny fabric pulled from Mama's sewing box. Papa would solemnly say a few comforting words; we girls would sing favorite songs and carefully bury the remains with a little cross to mark the grave and, of course, a spray of flowers picked from their beautiful garden.

One of the strangest pets we had growing up was a pollywog that I had caught while we were hiking around a little lake. We transferred him to his new home in a fish bowl that sat on top of our small organ. The pollywog grew and grew and, suddenly, began to sprout legs. Every day, we would run home to watch its metamorphosis. One day, we got home, and the fish bowl was empty. The whole family unsuccessfully searched the house to no avail. What a tragedy! There was not even a body to bury and, therefore, no funeral. Many months later, when Mama was spring cleaning and changing the furniture around, she moved the little organ away from the wall and found a very petrified dried-up dead frog who had made his first leap out of the safety of his fish bowl to the desert place behind the organ with no water or food available. We were hoping that he did not suffer and was able to use his new little legs at least for a short time.

When we moved away from Los Angeles and back to the country at Papa's first real church as pastor in Buttonwillow, California, the parsonage was right next door to the church and had a fenced-in backyard. Of course, the first thing on our agenda was to finally get a new dog. Again, with finances so tight, buying a puppy was out of the question. So one day, while we were in school, our parents took a thirty-mile road trip into Bakersfield to the dog pound. As they started in the door, they saw a lady with an ugly bowlegged little brown-and-white-spotted fox terrier. She said she could not keep her anymore because the other dogs picked on her. She carefully instructed our parents that the dog's name was Queenie. They could not help but giggle because she looked like anything but a queen. They adopted her on the spot and changed her name to Teenie, which seemed much more appropriate to her looks. The country air must have been a difficult adjustment to this city dog because she kept sneezing. Soon, they found, by offering a treat, she would sneeze on command when they said slowly "Teenie Sneeeeeze." She was a fast learner and soon had a repertoire of tricks to entertain and delight us.

Teenie in backyard at Buttonwillow ready for ride to town

During family devotions, she learned to put her front paws up on a chair, bow her head with paws folded, and growl until she heard "AMEN"! She danced in delight on her hind legs, going round and round until the music stopped, and of course, she learned usual tricks like: shake, sit, down, roll over, etc. The family delighted in showing off her repertoire to all visitors. As young girls, I am sure we often caused the poor dog much insult to her dignity by dressing her up in doll clothes, complete with hat and dark glasses, and taking her for rides around the neighborhood in our doll buggies. We even put her on top of the little lamb I was raising for 4H that lived in our backyard. She would balance on her back and ride around like a circus performer. She had amazing grace and patience with our requirements of her.

She became responsible for the first graphic demonstration of the facts of life when she became pregnant with her first litter of puppies. (A condition that occurred even with a chicken-wire-fenced backyard, vigilance by the family, and a protective little diaper Mama put on her when she went into heat.) As novice dog owners, we were not sure how long gestation was in dogs, but we were scheduled to go to Southern California to see our grandparents. Papa's church responsibilities did not leave a lot of time for trips, so even with Teenie's delicate condition, we all jumped in the car for the long road trip. When we got there, Mama was resting on the couch when, suddenly, the dog jumped up in her lap and proceeded to have her puppies. Mama quickly yelled for reinforcements, and other adults brought towels and water to facilitate the birthing process. We girls woke up to watch this amazing miracle. After a couple of hours, five little wiggly puppies were eagerly nursing. We were able to find wonderful homes for all of them in our church family, and we also had received our important first object lesson in biology.

This little dog moved several times with us from church to church. Her favorite "husband" was a Pomeranian across the street who managed to father her liters even with the family's watchful eye on her backyard business trips. One union even took place by her backing up to the fence holes. They were stuck together with a fence between them. One little runt we kept as a companion for her after we finally got her "fixed." We called him Bongo after one of our favorite stories of the circus bear. This little guy took after his father, with a ring of fluffy brown curly hair, but he had his mother's sweet patient disposition and unusual aptitude for learning tricks.

Many years later, when we girls were off to college, Teenie finally faced her last days on earth and left a huge hole in the family. She had seemed to have a little stroke and became unconscious as Papa raced his pickup the seven miles to town to the only vet, with her in his lap. He talked to her all the way, but before he could reach the vet's office, she roused enough to lick his hand and then died. Our tough Papa cried all the way back and then conducted a special funeral for our longest-living pet. Our parents always had a dog after that, but none of them were as special or talented as Teenie.

As we grew, we learned that God did not always promise us a rose garden, and that life was not always happiness abounding, but He did promise He would never leave us or forsake us but would be with us always through the valley of the shadow of death, walking with us or carrying us through the difficult situations of life. So regardless of the circumstances, we were confident that we could experience God's joy every day of our life.

Chapter 3

THE FRUIT OF THE SPIRIT IS LOVE, JOY...

PEACE

The completion of each day was an especially peaceful time in our lives. No matter how late it was or how much was on tomorrow's schedule, we had family devotions. We all gathered in our jammies around Papa's big chair for the scripture reading. Many times, we were allowed that reading privilege and, therefore, learned many big words as we read. We would try to sound new words out, and then if we could not get it, one of our parents would gently pronounce it correctly for us. The prayer time was always started with the youngest to the eldest. Oftentimes, all us children were sound asleep before Mama and Papa got through the many petitions and gratitude for blessings that they wanted to express to our heavenly Father. We would wake up briefly to the strains of our folks singing,

> Good night, our God is watching over you
> Good night, His mercy goes before you
> Good night, and we'll be praying for you
> So good night, may God bless you.

We first learned to harmonize by singing that little song each night. Then each parent would pick up a warm little body to tuck in for the night. This Good Night song followed into the next generation and the following one. It was even sung at the memorial services of our parents by all the kids, grandkids, and great grandkids.

Another very peaceful memory was Sunday night service that always ended with the little verse in Isaiah 26:3 set to a wonderful melody

> Thou wilt keep him in perfect peace whose
> mind is stayed on Thee.
> When the shadows come and darkness
> falls,

He giveth inward peace,
For He is the only perfect resting place,
He giveth perfect peace.
Thou wilt keep him in perfect peace whose
    mind is stayed on Him.

Prior to the end of the service, one of the ushers would turn off the house lights so only the cross was lighted and became our focus. What a wonderful way for the church family to start a new work week with a special reminder of Jesus who brings the *peace* that passeth all understanding.

No matter what type of problem or disaster fell into our young lives, we knew that our parents could handle it with God's help. We learned early not to be afraid of death. Funerals were an event to be anticipated with real peace. Many times, our family was called on to furnish the music for the funerals, especially if it was one of the church family. We learned early what a comfort that brings. Papa always gave Mama any honorarium that he received from funerals to use for special treats for the family. Sometimes, she would use it to take the family out to dinner at a nice restaurant (other than McDonalds or Foster Freeze) or she would get something special she needed for the house, or she might buy us a new store-bought dress or maybe just an ice cream at the soda fountain. Typically, the funerals were senior citizens who had lived a long life and had fought a good fight and finished their course. These services were more like a celebration home going. We learned early on that God knew we would grieve at the passing of a loved one, but we would not carry on like those with no hope. We were at one service where the mother fell on the casket screaming "NO!" and could hardly be restrained. Papa was quick to reassure us that people grieved in many ways, but our God was always there to comfort and sustain us.

We were never afraid of the coffin, for Papa always explained that the strange-looking, plastic-appearing cold body was just that person's "earth suit." The dead person was no longer contained there but was more alive than ever and resting in Heaven without any pain or sorrow. One of our favorite funeral stories Papa told was about Mama. When she was just twenty-two years old and still a novice in the ministry, she was scheduled for a tonsillectomy (in those days, the procedure was done in the doctor's little surgical room in the office). One of the church deacons, who had just retired and went from long hectic work weeks to sleeping in, with nothing really to occupy his time, died suddenly just a few weeks after retirement, and Mama was asked to sing "Sunrise Tomorrow" at the funeral. Rather than rescheduling the surgery, the doctor gave her a sedative to relax her and told her to come in right after the funeral. The music room was upstairs in that mortuary. Papa was downstairs helping with the funeral service. Mama started singing in her clear ethereal voice; all the congregation listened in awe as the beautiful song just floated through the room. The last few tones really floated and floated and floated: "Sunriseeeeeeeeeeeeeee." The song was never completed. Papa bolted up the stairs to catch her just before she hit the floor. He had to carry her downstairs virtually unresponsive, and then had a terrible time finding the physician's office since she had the only directions. (Obviously, this was before GPS, etc.) Mama remembers feeling like she was wrapped in cotton with lead feet. The tonsillectomy finally proceeded without further incident, but the impact of the last notes of the song long remained with the congregation.

We kids learned early in life how much difference there was in watching a saint of God being promoted from this earth to their *eternal* home in Heaven versus a family who lost its loved one with virtually no hope. For them, the last breath of this life was the real end of the story! This brought a sadness that could not be easily comforted. These were also Papa's most difficult funeral services. Many times, local morticians would call Papa to say the last words for a grieving family who were not affiliated with any church. He usually complied with the request, feeling that this was a rich opportunity to tell people of the "Peace that passeth all understanding"! (Some verses still sound better in the King James Version.)

Even cemeteries did not hold the fear for us that most children experienced. When we were very young, many of the funeral services were held at Forest Lawn. It was a beautiful park-like cemetery on a hill overlooking Los Angeles. There were many attractions that brought many tourists to the area as well, including a huge painting of the crucifixion. This was displayed in a large auditorium with spotlighted narration that vividly told about the events surrounding the death of Christ. We saw the program many times, and it helped us understand the sacrifice He made for us. After being a part of many memorial services, we realized the body being put in the ground was just a place for the "earth suit" to be stored after God had taken the real person to Heaven. While we were waiting for our parents to work with the family, we found it was interesting to read the tombstones and get a feeling of history that the person represented. Papa was very faithful to visit his own parents' graves with flowers, and he used it as an opportunity to tell about his family history and the impact these individuals had on our lives. Papa was the youngest in a family of four kids. They were his big sister and older twin brothers. One of them was an amazingly good child who developed and died from diabetes the year before insulin was developed. Papa always said, "God took him because he was too good to live in this earth."

Cultural differences at funerals really made a deep impression on us growing up. In those years, it was not unusual for families to keep their loved one at home, "laid out" for visitors to see and pay their respects. A positive response to this practice was allowing an actual transition time to occur, where families got used to the fact the person was no longer alive. There was time for lots of visiting and sharing past joys and experiences and always lots of food.

Our first experience with a black family's funeral was for a special preacher friend of Papa's. His church gave Papa the opportunity to share some words at the actual service. The open coffin was placed in the front of the church, with the old preacher's body outfitted in his best suit propped up for all to see. There was always a lot of soul-stirring gospel music like the "Saints Go Marching In" and other favorite songs repeated over and over. The service was not our traditional less than one hour that we were accustomed to sharing but a two- to three-hour "celebration of life." Music, including one of our special trios, shared memories, and lots of food were the order for the day.

Usually, for funeral's in our church family, the ladies in the fellowship always ensured that there was bountiful food to share after the burial service. Sometimes, there were strangers that came, either out-of-town family members or friends, so people did not question their appearance but made them welcome. However, Papa soon identified one elderly lady that seemed to show up at almost every funeral reception. She was not known to any one at the church, but they discovered that she lived near the building and realized that a great outing and super meal could be had by lining up and joining the funeral procession.

The first time I actually remember being with someone who died was when my paternal grandmother lost her battle with a difficult illness. We had all gathered at her house and were watching the ambulance attendants carry her out the door. She had been suffering so long there were permanent creases in her face. Suddenly, the pain and suffering were erased from her face, and she was at perfect peace. She said in a clear voice, "I see Jesus and His angels coming for me," and she took her last breath. What an impression on the young people in the family to see the difference being a Christian meant when facing death. "Let not your heart be troubled" and the rest of John 14 was permanently etched on my memory. It is very hard to stay afraid of an unknown like death when it is treated like a celebration of the saints going to be with their Lord in the eternal home He prepared for them. Not to say that we would not miss Grandma Whitaker's gentle spirit, but we had that assurance that we would see her again in Heaven.

Chapter 4

THE FRUIT OF THE SPIRIT IS LOVE, JOY, PEACE...

PATIENCE

As a parent now, I can hardly imagine how my own parents survived two very active little girls confined to bed for two years. In those days, the diagnosis of rheumatic fever was not well understood and was feared for its tragic after effects to the heart almost as much as polio. Our doctor did not even know how to treat it, except for bed rest and hot packs for the terrible leg cramps. Even the idea of keeping two little ones entertained while on enforced bed rest, without the benefit of television or movies, is astounding. Our little bed was covered with all the little Golden Books as well as Bible story adventures, and we quickly learned how to read. We also learned from them valuable life lessons such as "The Little Engine that Could." The phrase from that book actually became a family motto when we were faced with a difficult task. We would say, "I think I can, I think I can!" We learned to keep trying and never to give up no matter how hard the task appeared.

During the acute phase of our illness, our parents became very creative with methods to distract us from the discomfort and boredom we struggled with each day. Favorite board games were played over and over. We learned to make paper dolls with all their wardrobes, and we would act out stories on our beds. We made sock puppets and had them tell us their favorite stories. A time that we greatly anticipated was Saturday morning, when the radio would have the wonderful world of *Let's Pretend* and the antics of the *Buster Brown Shoes* show that featured "Clunk, Your Magic Clanger Froggie!" He brought all sorts of magical worlds for us to travel in our imaginations. The late afternoons and early evenings also were eagerly anticipated because of the entertainment of radio shows. *Fibber McGee and Molly*, the *Lone Ranger, Cisco Kid*, and Art Linkletter all became special friends as we were imprisoned on that bed or in the rocking chair all twenty-four hours of the day.

A home teacher helped us to keep up with or even slightly ahead of our grade. Finally, after two years, the illness ran its course, and we were released by the doctor to go to school. I started my own schooling without the benefit of kindergarten or first and second grade. The time and work invested by our parents and the home teacher really paid off, and I was jump started into the thick of things in third grade. So much reading while we were sick gave us foundational knowledge that made elementary school more fun that work. Our first school was six blocks away, and the streets were dark with overgrown trees shading them. Shady Lane created a fearful atmosphere that usually had us running the whole distance, thinking something scary would pounce on us from the trees any minute. It did not help our anxiety when Mama had to teach us what to do if we were snatched by someone, after the school had sent warnings home about strangers hanging around the playground fence. We learned that many people in the world were truly evil, so it was best to stay close to our friends while walking to and from school.

Although our parents' schedules were packed by the demands of school, church, and other jobs, they always patiently found time to listen to our problems, share our distresses, and help us to learn ways to problem solve with anticipatory thinking. They made flash cards for those pesky multiplication tables, and we soon learned to answer each problem with ease. Maybe because of the two-year enforced inactivity, we had difficulty sitting still when the activity restrictions were removed. Our little bodies wanted to be in constant motion. Our grandfather promptly dubbed us "wiggle warts." This was a title that stuck for many years.

Long trips were common in our childhood. It took several hours to get to each of our grandparents' residences on those special holidays like Christmas or for their birth-days. Going across Los Angeles was difficult for there were not many freeways in those days. We also had to make trips to nearby towns for necessary church meetings. Papa had to often remind himself to exercise patience in those travel situations. We would be barely a few blocks from home, and he would be entreated with "When are we going to get there?" or even more frustrating, "I have to go potty." Mama was ahead of the "I'm hungry" cry for she had boxes of animal crackers stashed away for us. Once, in total frus-tration after hearing "when are we going to get there" too many times from the back seat, he decided that he would add that phrase to my name: "Nancy When Are We Going To Get There Whitaker."

No matter the length of the trip, they would start sing-ing: "There's a hole in the bottom of the sea" or "Found a Peanut." We learned the books of the Bible easily by song. I still find I can learn Bible verses more easily when they are set to music. It put their mental gymnastics to work to keep us occupied with stimulating games. The miles rolled past and the hours ticked by and we would be another step closer toward learning a degree of patience.

Later, growing up, we learned that patience develops in an interesting way. The Bible says trials bring patience. So if we prayed for patience in a certain situation, Papa gently reminded us "be careful what you pray for." All of us seemed to have a little more trouble with this fruit of the Spirit. Papa would often recite, "Patience is a virtue, possess it if you can, always found in women and rarely found in man." He could get away with that one in an all-girl house. That also became his excuse for asking us to hurry up when we needed to get moving to be on time for an appointment. Being sadly outnumbered in an all-girl house, Papa had to develop real patience waiting for his turn in the bathroom. In all of our growing up years, there was only one bathroom in the houses we lived. Most of the time, he had to waken early to grab first dibs on the hot water for shaving. As we got older and seemed to correspondingly take longer to get ready, Papa had to develop shower guidelines. We learned a shower really could be taken in just three minutes, and our bedrooms worked just as well for putting on makeup or doing our hair.

A little immigrant lady who came to our church had never eaten corn on the cob before. She ate her first piece with gusto and then held out the cob and said, "Would you please put more beans on my stick?" Papa loved that phrase so much that, from then on, he incorporated it whenever he wanted seconds of anything. Sometimes, Mama almost lost her patience when hearing the same phrase over and over again. The first few times, it might have been funny, but after hearing it multiple times, the humor was lost for her, and her patience was gone.

My hair was reddish and extremely curly. Mama found the best way to handle it was to keep is very short. She used to call it my wash-and-wear hair since it only needed to be towel dried and then fluffed a bit. The process certainly shortened the getting-ready time, however, I envied my little sister whose hair was long and straight as a stick. It could be pulled into cute pigtails or French braided, but it took a long time and some crying to get the hair rescued from the tangled birds nest it became every night. Over the years, I began to appreciate how much easier my short hair was to handle. It was always a long ordeal when Mama had to give Linda a permanent. In those days, home permanents were not very reliable and certainly smelled up the house. The curlers pulled her hair as they worked diligently to catch all the flyaway strands. When I would complain about my curls, Mama would remind me of all the work involved with long hair and also reminded me that God did not make mistakes when he made us. Mama definitely exhibited the "patience of Job" while trying to get her little girls ready for the day's adventures. We are sure that she breathed a big sigh of relief when we proved that we could dress ourselves appropriately and take care of our own hygiene. Her need for patience in these areas was greatly diminished, and life became a little easier.

Chapter 5

THE FRUIT OF THE SPIRIT IS LOVE, JOY, PEACE, PATIENCE...

KINDNESS

During our childhood, our parents really protected us from the ugly or bad influences that were increasingly evident in our world. We only were able to read the funnies in the *Sunday Times*, and we did not own a television set. So the world's tragedies and horror were kept at bay in our home.

They knew that we would face enough of those problems as we grew up. At the Hollywood house, we had some lovely neighbors down the block who actually owned a television. Their girls would invite us down after homework was done to watch Shirley Temple movies and Beanie and Cecil the Seasick Sea Serpent. Usually, their mom would have little treats for us to enjoy as well. The girls then came to our house for our parents Good News Club, which taught the neighborhood kids the Good News of the Gospel. They also introduced us to ice skating at the Polar Palace. After a vigorous workout, their parents would allow us to get a vanilla or chocolate ice cream soda at the fountain. These special Saturday morning adventures gave our parents a very necessary break. Ice skating was a skill we enjoyed throughout our lifetime. Papa even made a little ice rink out of the patio at the cabin so we could skate whenever it was freezing. I even used ice skating as my required two years of PE during college. The memories of those special days remain with us to this day. Even though many miles now separate us from those girls, they remain great "first friends"!

A fundamental precept that our parents exhibited was the verse "Be ye kind one to another." Mama defined this in many ways, but one of her most utilized was "if you can't say something nice, do not say anything at all." She always taught us to look for the best in others, and if there was conflict, be sure and return ugly behavior with kindness. From this wisdom, we learned that how you approach someone can definitely make a difference in the outcome of conflict. Long before the business and professional world began teaching the importance of initiating contact with those you meet in a positive way with a smile and "good morning," we learned kind behavior goes a long way to diffuse a hostile environment.

The dictionary defines kindness as "good or benevolent nature or disposition, compassionate, considerate, and helpful." All of these characteristics could be used in describing our parents. They were the ultimate in hospitality. Our door was always open for someone who needed a place to stay or a hot meal. Mama always made enough dinner on Sunday for extra guests. All of us girls understood MIK (more in kitchen), which was code for "eat all you want for there is plenty for all." It was not unusual for Papa to bring home a family who had been stranded when their car broke down, or they ran out of money for gas to get them to their destination. In those days, the church filled a huge hole of meeting social service needs. People knew if they could get to a church, they would receive help.

However, right and wrong were very much "black and white" in our home. We quickly learned it was not wise to cross the line. When there were grey areas or a problem that did not seem so easy to solve, we were taught to ask ourselves "What would Jesus do?" This spilled over even into social dilemmas when our school friends were going somewhere where alcohol was served or there was not sufficient adult supervision. Our parents would say, "Would you think Jesus would be comfortable in that setting?"

Acts of unkindness were not tolerated and brought quick retribution to the offenders. Long before "time outs" were popular for discipline, our parents used the fought-over toy or game as the "time out," and it would not be available for play until we could share nicely. We learned to appreciate all of the blessings God had given to us and to cherish the other creations He made for us to enjoy. Sometimes, the work of a Saturday afternoon would be arrested as we all lay down on the grass to watch lovely white billowing clouds float by. We would use our overactive imaginations to see how many different pictures of animals or birds we could define in the cloud formations. No matter how many deadlines were facing them or anxieties they gracefully hid, our parents always had time for us to stop and point out the amazing beauty of God's creation.

Papa enjoying his beautiful roses

One of Mama's true pleasures in life were beautiful flowers, so Papa worked very hard to be sure she was surrounded with them. A positive element for him was that he found gardening was a good way to relax from the stresses and responsibilities of his job. He was especially proud of his bulbs and cultivated many beautiful rows of dahlias, iris, daffodils, etc. One day, as I was riding my bike down the sidewalk next to his garden strip, he turned around to see a beautiful blossom hit the ground. He assumed that I had run over it with my bike wheel and reacted quickly to that offense. However, while we were standing there discussing the transgression, another beautiful flower hit the ground just like it had been cut off with a knife. Papa picked up the poor flowers, and we went for a drive to the nearby nursery. Papa was told by the gardener that this was the work of a cutworm and definitely not a bike wheel. He immediately apologized for his conclusion jumping and asked forgiveness for his response. He learned a valuable lesson that day too, that circumstances aren't always what they seem.

The Golden Rule became one of our family guidelines. We learned how to use our ten fingers to remember the words of the verse, "As ye would that men should do to you, do ye also to them likewise" (King James Version). The remarkable thing about this lesson was that we saw it really worked. Whether it was a disagreement on the playground over game rules, a neighborhood bully trying to have his own way, or sisters claiming ownership of the same toy, when we tried to think how we would want to be treated, we found a way to treat others that same way. Mama and Papa needed to reinforce this particular lesson many times before they became part of our natural response. My hair wasn't red for nothing! My natural response was to react rather than think it through. Many times, my thoughtless angry words or actions ended up escalating the situation so that it required a "board of education to the seat of learning" to reinforce that everything in life requires kindness.

In those days, the ministry was not listed as one of the professions that would bring financial gain. Even though Papa had thirteen years of schooling past high school, this education was not rewarded financially, and his salary was usually just above minimum wage. During the real tight economic times, Mama learned to make much out of nothing. We had lovely Sunday dresses made from feed sacks from Grandpa's farm trimmed with beautiful lace or elegant ribbon that she would retrieve from other people's cast offs. Most of our clothing was made without benefit of patterns. Mama had the uncanny talent of just looking at something and being able to duplicate the intricacies. The missionary baskets were another source of our clothing wardrobes. There were real treasures to be found there that were discarded by children who had outgrown them or no longer cared for the styles. The church ladies made certain that we had first dibs on any item of clothing that fit before it was sent on for processing by the mission committee. At the time, we never realized that our parents often went without necessities to make sure we had the extra little nice things that we longed to have.

Mama often entertained us by telling about our early days when we had very little actual memories of the events that transpired. Toward the completion of the Second World War, Papa was music and youth director at Asbury Methodist Church in San Diego. Since San Diego was a huge navy and marine base, the church began a very active ministry for the servicemen, including a servicemen's center where enlisted men were able to mingle with officers. There was a gym with basketball and volleyball courts, a great library, board games, and many structured activities.

Papa and other men from church would drive down to Balboa Park, pick up as many servicemen as they could load up in their cars and bring them back for a day spent with church families. The women from church would save their ration stamps to buy Salisbury steak for a delicious dinner for the fellows who attended church. Sometimes, it was a little difficult for any of the congregation to concentrate on the sermon when the tantalizing aroma of cooking food drifted up from the church kitchen. Often, we had servicemen on leave spending the weekend on our couch or even curled up on the rug, just starving for a taste of family life that they left behind to serve their country. There are many pictures of us girls being held or played with by the guys in uniform. Some of them were still close friends of our parents until they went to Heaven. The men often repeated how much their kindness meant to them during those very difficult war years.

WWII San Diego

Mama's creativity hanging up hundreds of
Christmas cards remembering dear friends

Our Grandpa Whitaker when he moved in
with them after losing Grandma

Kindness was an attribute they exemplified all through
their lives. During papa's last church in Corning, California,
his father sold his own house in Southern California and
came up to visit with them. It was too hard with Grandma
gone, and his advancing age meant increased difficulties
dealing with traffic. I remember going with him to the gro-
cery store to pick up discarded old produce for his chick-
ens. He pulled up to the signal in the middle lane, but then
realized he needed to turn left. When the left turn signal
came, he joined the lane turning. A policeman thought this
was not right and put on his red light to pull him over.
He said, "Can't you see you were not in the correct lane
to turn left?" Grandpa said, "Of course, I can see," and he

pulled out a copy of the small-print vehicle code to read the first page. The policeman did not know he had this page memorized, and he let him off the hook again. Papa used to tell us his father could talk his way out of a paper bag. Grandpa's little visit became permanent, and he decided the little house on the hill was where he wanted to live his last days. He helped with the garden and milked the goats. He did well except when they found out the reason their cat was getting so fat was Grandpa fed her every time he woke up from a nap and thought it was a new day. The poor cat almost exploded from his tender care.

He did not let grass grow under his feet here he is with new
wife Melvina (one of Papa's deaconnesses and 18 years younger
with papa & Mama, Linda and her Baby Scotty)

He was ninety years old when he began to court a little deaconess from Papa's church who was a mere seventy-two years old. We girls asked him how it felt dating a woman who was born when he was already eighteen years old. He said that, at their advanced years, age does not matter. We were amazed that our Papa took the time to be their own private chauffeur for their dates. He even arranged to pick up the flowers and candy that Grandpa had to have for the special times. Soon, they were planning a wedding, and our parents realized the old couple would need some privacy yet availability for any emergency. In typical Papa fashion, he quickly traced out a modification to the garage that included a furnished sitting room, small kitchen, bedroom, and bath. He even rigged a baby monitor so they could get help fast if needed. He worked day and night to complete the job before the big wedding. They were grateful for their little apartment that even accessed the back garden. The family had many years of enjoying their stories and wisdom before God called them home. Grandma Melvina was treasured by the whole family as the best apple-pie maker in the universe. We girls tried to learn the secret of the perfect flaky crust and watched every move, but she said to our many requests for the recipe, "You just feel when it is the right amount"! She was very quiet and reserved but also very adept at putting up with the chaos that resulted from all of us gathering together for holidays or special celebrations. Our parents always tried to demonstrate to us in very meaningful ways what acts of kindness really meant in the lives of the people they served. From early years, we made hospital visits with them or sat with them at the bedside of a shut-in, reading and singing to help them through the difficult journey. These times made deep impressions on our minds of what the verse expressed, "it is more blessed to give than to receive." We knew that those visits brought us more awareness of the challenges of life. We learned that happiness does not come from possessions or wealth but from seeing smiles on the faces of those in need of encouragement. Whatever was required of them in the ministry, they did with their whole hearts. Their theme song was

> Every work for Jesus will be blessed, but
> He asks of everyone their best.
> Our talents may be small, but unto Him
> is due our best our all!

This philosophy was passed on to their children and grandchildren by constant example and expectations.

Chapter 6

THE FRUIT OF THE SPIRIT IS LOVE, JOY, PEACE, PATIENCE, KINDNESS...

GOODNESS

We learned in school that the definition of goodness was "moral excellence that refers to a general quality recognized inherent or a part of one's basic character." A synonym might be virtue. However, we kids learned what that word actually met by watching our parents handling the everyday problems of life. No matter what was happening, they always went the extra mile for everyone. The door was truly open day or night. Visitors were welcomed and made comfortable no matter what time was on the clock. Everything they had was shared with others. As children, we never knew when we were tucked in at night what we would find in the morning. There might be a family unable to find a motel, a drunk who passed out on the corner and Papa rescued before he was taken to the jail's drunk tank, or a visiting missionary who found our house after getting lost in the California traffic.

It was very difficult for us to understand other reactions, especially when we were older and ran into situations with friends whose parents would say "I'm sorry we cannot help. It is past time for us to retire for the evening." The spirit of hospitality was always awake and ready at *our house no matter* what time it was or how much they desired to sleep. Anyone in the congregation or neighborhood with a need knew that the help of our parents was only a phone call away. Many nights, they spent praying and encouraging anxious families waiting for news from the emergency room or surgical suite regarding a critical loved one. The demands of the ministry would really have taken a toll on their health if they were not blessed with wisdom to escape for wonderful vacations when needed. Some of our earliest *memories are of the times* of rest and recreation we had camping, hiking, swimming, boating, and generally enjoying God's beautiful outdoors.

Mama on her air mattress so relaxed (but no sun screen) :(
She paid for it with many lesions biopsied and resected in later years

The ocean and the mountains were our favorite des-
tinations. Occasionally, we were invited to stay at friends'
cabins, which felt like a piece of Heaven. One of these
friends had a "beautiful cabin" that was both mountains
and ocean combined, near the town of Cambria Pines by
the sea. The draw for us was not the woods or the ocean
but a wooden swing that hung from a huge pine tree on
a slope, so the swing out was a huge drop below. To this
day, I can hear Mama yelling "hold on tight," but she did
not forbid us to try this exciting challenge. It is the clear-
est memory we have of that cabin. Another favorite cabin
was just below Lake Arrowhead. Woody Gwynn was one of

the sailors they had befriended during the war. He married one of the church girls, and they became lifelong friends of our parents. They planned many wonderful trips together after all retired. One of Mama's favorite things was just paddling around on an air mattress on the quiet lake. As we learned to swim, more air mattresses were packed so all of us could enjoy that fun. Remember, this was before the development of sunscreen, and to their consternation, the all-day paddling left a bad result on their fair child—second-degree burns on my back and legs. Neither of them had medical training but found that wet towels seemed to help soothe the burns. They learned the hard way that I needed protection from the sun. With all my freckles, Papa used to say that I got all my suntan through a screen door.

One memorable summer, we had a graphic geography lesson about the USA, when Papa and Mama saved for a new reliable car and took us, along with our maternal grandfather, on an unforgettable coast-to-coast, south-to-north trip across most of the forty-eight states. Much of the time, we were able to stay with relatives or with one of the many friends they had from the ministry. A few times, we were caught with too many miles between planned stops. The solution was for us girls to sleep snugly on the seats of the car, while our parents and Grandpa Stark would bed down in sleeping bags next to the car. One mission station we stayed in was at an Indian reservation in New Mexico. We had a firsthand lesson on how the original native populations lived. Their beautiful creativity and use of color was amazing. While there, we visited our great-uncle in Taos, New Mexico, who introduced us to a local tribe of Indians who believed stealing was only wrong if you got caught. Therefore, they wore all of their clothing in layers all the time. They also never left anything of value in their hogans, for when they had to leave, everything would be gone on their return. They had embraced the modern dress of the time by buying Levis, but they would cut the bottoms out and still use their blankets to cover them. Their love was baseball, but due to their impoverished condition, they could not afford the admission price for a ticket to the game. However, everyone there could see their vividly colored blankets and, at times, their bare bottom perched on the tree limbs surrounding the field.

Uncle Albert in New Mexico after fixing venison stew for the
game warden asking about hearing (out of season) gunshots

Papa's uncle had always been a renegade explorer and probably considered by the neighbors as a real eccentric "crazy old duffer," but to us, he was Daniel Boone and Wild Bill Hickock rolled into one. He loved the mountains and hunting and fishing in his Red River Valley, but he had little tolerance for the rules and regulations that the encroaching civilization brought with them. The local game wardens knew him well. When they heard the report of a rifle out of hunting season, they could quickly identify the source. Uncle would calmly answer their questions about out-of-season deer hunting by offering them a bowl of mouthwatering venison stew. It seems that even the local law officials were willing to overlook his hunting out of season for a good hearty dinner.

As California girls, we were not used to the torrential rains and violence of electrical storms common in the Midwest. One night in Kentucky, we had fallen asleep next to a school bus shelter, so the adults would be sleeping out of the rain that was threatening. In the middle of the night, a loud crash brought me out of a deep sleep. My sister had always been a very heavy sleeper, but I could not believe she could sleep through the noise of that tremendous thunder or the sky lit up with lightning flashes. I could not see her breathing and was convinced she was dead, probably struck by the huge lightning bolts. My shrieks of terror, "Linda's dead, Linda's dead," quickly brought all the adults up to see what had happened. They comforted me and demonstrated that my little sister really could sleep through anything. The next day, we were able to find our real destination, a mission orphanage run by one of Papa's college friends from Biola. We spent several days there, seeing all the work they were doing in those isolated hills. The children rapidly assimilated us into their work and games.

They could have fun with just the smallest items such as a tin can for the game kick the can. Although only with them a short time, we left with the Kentucky Hills accent sprinkled throughout our speech. Pictures of the poverty, tumbledown shacks, and mountain grandmothers rocking on their front porches with their corncob pipes will always be forever etched in our memories.

Our parents were dedicated to making this trip a treasured memory, so we stopped at every national park, cave, historic landmark, and special roadside attraction that we came by. We were able to visit Mt Vernon, Washington, DC, with the Capitol, White House, Lincoln and Washington memorials, and the solemnity of the Arlington Cemetery. The Civil War came alive for us when we reached Gettysburg, with its rows and rows of graves and monuments. Each day was a new chapter in our land's history. Our parents really sacrificed to give us a wonderful glimpse of the nation they loved. We also enjoyed a blessed opportunity to listen for hours to the wisdom and stories of our grandpa, who could also find a joke about anything. He was adept at saying one-line jokes that would put us all into gales of laughter, and in his honor, we dubbed all those jokes "Starkies." As little kids, we were not privy to the problems of the trip. Grandpa was suffering from prostate cancer and had to make frequent stops to relieve himself. Sometimes, with no bathroom available, he found a tree. While going over the mountains, we had to drive carefully through leftover snow. We made snowcones with vanilla and sugar poured over the snow, a real yummy treat. Grandpa, after making a quick trip to a tree, made sure we understood never to eat "yellow" snow!

One of our favorite things was seeing the massive faces of Papa's favorite presidents at Mount Rushmore: Abraham Lincoln, George Washington, Theodore Roosevelt, and Thomas Jefferson. We had difficulty understanding how someone could carve their likeness in correct proportions on the face of those cliffs without the help of computers or other technical assistance. It is also hard to understand how Papa negotiated through the many states we covered without the help of a GPS or cell phone. While going through an isolated area in the northwest, Papa had his only "accident," a pheasant flew up right into the hood of the car, killing it instantly.

Papa went over to check the damage and was joined by a game warden who asked, "What are you going to do with that bird?"

Papa said, "Maybe have him for dinner?"

The game warden replied, "You do and I will sock you with a $500 fine. Those birds are protected!"

Papa always wondered if a yummy pheasant under glass dinner was a side benefit for the hardworking warden. However, it was the end of our potential pheasant dinner! It is still very difficult for us to even imagine taking a trip of this magnitude on very limited funds with five people, and all there in a car for that length of time. The only time we stayed in a motel was in Washington, DC, because our parents wanted us all to be cleaned up and at our very best for seeing the Nation's capital.

Trip to Tijuana with big sister Judy and her friends
with Mama, baby Linda, and Nancy

The whole family participated in Sister
Judy's wedding to her sailor Russ

Papa with his Aunt Iva another family member who
lived with us a while after her husband died

As we were growing up, there was always someone who
needed a family that joined us for a period of time. The first
was our "big sister Judy," a young girl from the San Diego
church who had lost her parents. Her grandmother wasn't
able to care for her and her sister, so she lived with us from
age twelve to eighteen, when she was married. Although
never formally adopted legally, she became our big sister in every way. She always said she was the model that
taught our parents how to deal with teenagers. After her
marriage, she moved into a little beach house on Mission

Beach. Our parents would pack our things and put us on the train for a visit every summer. We learned many valuable lessons from her on keeping a house, especially when her three girls arrived. Next moving in to the Hollywood house was Papa's Aunt Iva, who had just lost her husband and needed a place to live. She was a godsend since Mama had to work at Ralph's Market and then as a PBX operator for the Southern California Gas Company. Her extra hard work helped pay the bills while Papa finished seminary. Aunt Iva functioned as chief cook and bottle washer until we moved to Buttonwillow in 1952. Next to move in with them was Grandpa Whitaker and his new wife in Corning. They were joined by Mama's older sister, Nellie, who had an extremely odd disease and needed constant physical care until she died. When they moved to Washington after retiring from full-time ministry, Mama's other sister came for a two-week visit that morphed into ten years. Through it all, with all the chaos and comings and goings, Papa and Mama faced it all with goodness.

After Papa resigned from West Hollywood Baptist due to a difficult but very necessary surgery, we moved to the cabin at Hume Lake for the summer to give him time to recover. When summer was over, he was still not ready to go to work full-time at a new church, but there were no schools in those days in the mountains. It was a real dilemma for them, until the Warkentines offered to let us both stay with their family at the ranch in the valley. Walt and Frances Warkentine had known Papa since Biola school days as well as working together for camps at Hume Lake. They cheerfully took on two more teenagers, along with their own two teenage girls and a seven-year-old. Poor

Walt had to contend with six females in the home. Some days, the estrogen levels must have been seriously high!

Although our parents missed us and all the experiences we were having, Mama always called the time we spent with the Warkentine family our finishing school. Frances taught us so much about etiquette, being responsible for chores (the list was posted in the kitchen, and duties rotated each week), and how to successfully work together as a team. She always demonstrated the epitome of hospitality and goodness. We were able to go with the older girls to Immanuel Academy in Reedley. We never knew how our tuition was paid. Our parents certainly did not have the funds. They kept in touch even without cell phones and made sure we had the necessities for school, including nice dresses for the junior banquet.

During our stay there, we also enjoyed learning about the Mennonite heritage, history, and culture from Grandmother Hofer, who lived on a ranch on the next road, and others of the church family.

At that time, in the little country church, the men sat on one side and the women on the other with the kids in back. Their special food was a real delight. They definitely had a corner on the market in the pie-making department and other amazing desserts. Often, Grandmother Hofer would bring Nucala soup, which is similar to gnocchi, or she would share the amazing delicacy zwieback, which was like a double dinner roll that literally melted in your mouth.

We girls felt so comfortable with their family because we had a long history with them from summer adventures at Hume Lake. We rode horses, hiked up Sunshine Mountain and all the other nearby peaks, learned to drive in Grandpa's old '39 Ford, swam at Ten Mile Creek, had many overnighters, and worked on the summer staff. We even comforted each other through the agonies of teenage broken hearts. They were like having more sisters in our family. Each night, Nancy, who cheerfully shared her bedroom with me, and I would go to sleep listening to "Stan's Private Line" as we heard the familiar words every night:

> *Dream, when you're feeling blue, Dream,*
> *   that's the thing to do.*
> *Just watch the smoke rings rise in the air,*
> *   you'll find your share of memories there.*
> SO *dream when the day is through, dream*
> *   and they might come true,*
> *Things never are as bad as they seem, so*
> *   dream, dream, dream.*

Working on staff Hume Lake

Hume Lake Staff

We had a great time together dancing the polka in the front yard, giving elephant rides down the long hall to the little sister, and sharing the intricacies of beginning dating. We shared much laughter and a few tears, but I do not remember any catfights or disagreements. During the school year, Papa regained his strength and accepted the pastorate at Hanford Lakeside Baptist Church. We, as a family, will always appreciate the sacrifice their family made to help us through that difficult time. We girls have remained friends through the decades.

While we were growing up, Sunday lunches were always a special mealtime. There was always company invited to join us. It might have been a new family that just came to church for the first time, a visiting missionary, special speaker, or someone who had just suffered devastating loss of their spouse. Usually, Mama would be up very early to have her own devotions as she started a delicious pot roast with potatoes, onions, and carrots. She always tried to put more names in the pot than just our family and stretch the food budget as far as possible. A jello salad with fruit such as pineapple usually went a long way. At times, good old Bisquik allowed her to make muffins or biscuits to add to the feast. When food was limited, or more people showed up than what she had anticipated, we would be served last and knew not to ask for more unless Mama said the inside code MIK (which meant More in the Kitchen.). We learned much about our world while listening to the interesting conversations that occurred around the dinner table. We also learned valuable lessons of service as we took on more responsibility for the cleanup. We found that even doing dishes was fun when the work was shared, and we sang our way to the last pot scrubbed.

Occasionally, to Mama's chagrin, Papa would spice up the mealtime with little pranks on the honored guests. He collected coffee mugs with surprises in the bottom that could not be seen until the coffee was gone. One favorite contained a small ceramic frog, while another had a little mouse with cheese. Another of his favorite tricks if the dinners got too stuffy was to place a small air bladder on a long tube with a bulb under the tablecloth to be under a visitor's fancy water glass. If the conversation started lagging, the glass would suddenly tip back and forth precariously. It was hard for us to keep a straight face as guests wondered if there was an earthquake happening, after all, it was California.

When Papa's churches were in the country, like Buttonwillow or Hanford, we were able to have farm animals like little goats or lambs as pets. Papa often thought nothing of trotting one of them into the dining room for guests to greet. Sometimes, he would even feed them a bottle as Mama would almost melt in embarrassment. One of our frequent visitors was an evangelist friend who stayed with us whenever he was traveling through the area. He always tried to outprank our Papa. They started writing letters on increasingly outrageous paper. The last straw was when Papa received a note written on toilet paper. How could that one be topped? We soon found out as Papa smeared little bits of mustard on pieces of toilet paper and sent his reply scribbled between the stains. The last time we had a visit from this special friend, he left his thanks written in toothpaste on the bathroom mirror.

All visits from this special friend were always highly anticipated, not only for his jokes and "can you top this pranks" with Papa but also for his amazing musical ability. He could play almost any tune requested but topped his own accomplishments by being able to play two songs (one with each hand) at the same time. Often, this was done with different keys and, of course, different rhythms. It was an amazing gift that I've never seen duplicated, even by renowned entertainers on television.

Chapter 7

THE FRUIT OF THE SPIRIT IS LOVE, JOY PEACE, PATIENCE, KINDNESS, GOODNESS...
FAITHFULNESS

One of the most important lessons we learned about faith was threefold: God's faithfulness to us, the importance of our faith in Him, and being faithful in all our service to Him.

During the time of Papa's first pastorate in Buttonwillow, we became acquainted with Hume Lake Christian Camps. Often, we would spend our vacations there in camp as our parents counseled or were deans of youth camps. They grew to love that mountain retreat and, to our joy, purchased one of the lots above the camp to build a cabin. Even from Los Angeles, we would make the long road trip to Hume Lake for our cherished vacations. Usually, Papa would want us packed and ready to leave immediately after Sunday night service so not to waste even one moment of precious time in the mountains. It was a seven- to eight-hour trip to get up there. Papa was never really concerned about the state of our gas supply, for he felt confident that God would certainly provide for us.

As was their habit, especially since the reach of radio stations could not be relied on, we usually sang camp songs all the way until we could not keep our eyes open any longer. One by one, we would succumb to the need for sleep. One of our favorite songs became our family's hiking song. To the tune of "Long Long Trail," we sang:

> There's a long, long nail a grinding into
>   the sole of my shoe.
> It's ground its way into my foot a mile or
>   two.
> There's a long, long trail before me, here's
>   what I'm thinking about.
> The time that I can sit right down and
>   pull that dern nail out!

I am sure the author of that beautiful song would turn over in his grave to see how we had changed its message.

However, it really helped us make it up big hills or complete long hikes.

One trip, however, really brought that faith in God's provision as a searing memory. We were getting short of fuel and had passed many closed gas stations in the small towns along the valley on Highway 99. Suddenly, our parents realized we had started up the mountains with the tank registering nearly empty. We prayed hard that God would stretch the gas. Mama reminded us that if God could refill the widow's jars of oil during Elisha's time, He could surely multiply something as light as gasoline. Papa would calm our anxiety with the statement that God's guardian angels would push us up the hill to the top so we

Grandpa Stark working on rock chimney

could coast down to Hume. As we watched in disbelief, it seemed the gas gauge was stuck, and we made it farther and farther up the hill. The indicator had said EMPTY for some time, but Papa was convinced the angels were pushing us. Somehow, that must have happened because we made it all the way to the bottom of our street, Christmas Tree Lane. The miracle of Jesus multiplying the loaves and fishes seemed very real to us that night.

Grandma Stark, Mama, Nancy, & kids from cabin above us working
on the roof (since cabin was on a hill we were about 20 feet up

Every summer for several years, we worked our vacation time building the cabin. Grandpa Stark came to help
us many vacation periods. He was an amazing carpenter
and helped in every aspect of the building, from cellar to
the roof. It was not unusual to see the old man, mother and
father and both kids hanging onto the rafters while nailing
shingles thirty feet in the air. Papa used everything to make
that cabin. He rescued discarded sinks, toilets, pipes, and
electrical items to reduce the cost. One of the men in our
West Hollywood church was a contractor and gave him
many of his discards and leftovers from his own construction sites. Some of the wood that was used in the cabin
was part of the last trees milled from the old Hume Lake
sawmill. However, most of the supplies had to be hauled
up from the valley one trailer load at a time.

Until the cabin's skeleton was in place, we all found a special place to camp on the lot. Grandpa utilized an old set of springs with a tarp between a grove of trees for his bedroom. We girls instantly claimed a little group of trees on the top of the hill as our special room. We had all kinds of space among the branches to store our toys, books, and other treasures. We slept under the stars, and the sounds of nature were our lullaby each night. Our outdoor bedroom became a popular place with the other staff kids at Hume. We ended up having many slumber parties over the vacation times, and the Whitaker almost cabin became their home away from home.

One morning, Papa awakened early in their little tent to see a mother deer standing at the entrance. When she saw him move, she was startled and jumped sideways into the air about ten feet. He could hardly believe her dexterity and desire to protect her little spotted fawn. The deer became welcome visitors when they saw we would leave our dinner leftovers on the rock wall for them to feast upon. They usually came every evening through the back patio. One time, when Grandpa Whitaker was making an infrequent visit, he looked forward to the deer's visits and would offer them whatever he was eating. Our family could hardly believe it when we saw him feeding a deer from the makeshift kitchen right from his spoon. He was saying, "You a bite, me a bite." The most remarkable thing was the menu that afternoon was chili beans. That poor deer probably had a real stomachache to contend with after sharing that meal with Grandpa.

Mama's top priority for the cabin was the bathroom! Mainly, her goal was to get a private flushing toilet. After several summers of an outhouse only, Papa finally got the floor installed for the back corner of the cabin. The first fixture was the toilet, and he masterfully got it plumbed in. However, there were no walls yet, so it left privacy as a real problem. They were able to solve that by draping an old blue bedspread encircling the toilet. From that time on, we called it "the blue room," even after the walls were completed. Later, people never did understand when we would say we had to go to the "blue room." The bathroom was really never completed, although Papa did add a tub and sink over the years.

Swimming at 10 Mile creek after working at the cabin all morning

We usually worked all morning on the cabin, and then Mama and kids were released to the lake or Ten Mile Creek for a wonderfully restorative afternoon of swimming. Papa always was a little anxious when we were swimming. He could not get over his fear of water that originated from seeing his childhood friend drown in a mill pond. He hated to see us get in over our heads and would call us back saying, "You can swim just as good in three feet of water as you can in six feet." As we got older, we were able to do afternoon adventures on our own. The mountain became our refuge, and we hiked every peak and valley around it. One of our favorite hikes was up to the Little Brown Church. The Hume Conference had established a little meditation area over a lookout we called Inspiration Point, on the very top of the mountain ridge. The Little Brown Church was very little, about two feet tall. It contained a Bible and a logbook in which visitors could write about their "mountaintop experience" and special times with God. It was always very uplifting to read. It also became a very special sacred place to us. In the future, it was the location where my love asked me to marry him. It was also the place of tears and contriteness as we got ourselves back on a right spiritual plane. Later, the little church became the place our children sought refuge from the crises of their worlds.

The cabin became a destination for many of the church families. One time, the high school kids from West Hollywood came to stay for the high school camp. Our parents promptly put the girls in the sleeping loft upstairs and the boys in the basement. They were in the bedroom of the main floor as a physical barrier to any potential get-togethers. The high school boys asked to stay one extra day at the cabin. Without having any parental supervision, they started really horsing around. As boys play often, it continued to escalate until a whole hog pillow fight evolved. The pillows were flying across the cabin, and the boys were having a great time, until one old feather pillow burst under the stress. Suddenly, there were feathers all over the cabin.

Try as they would, they could not seem to corral them all. There were feathers on the open rafters, on the tops of all the furniture, window sills, etc. It looked like an indoor snowstorm. For years after that, feathers would come floating down from the rafters as a reminder of that memorable pillow fight.

The feathers were also a reminder of one of Papa's favorite illustrations about gossip. A lady who had the infamous reputation as the church gossip had spread wild stories that hurt someone very badly. In true contrition, she went to the pastor, asking how she could make amends. He told her to take a feather pillow to the church belfry, open the end, and scatter the feathers to the four winds. She did that but did not feel any better. He then told her, "Now you need to go and pick them all up again." That was an amazing example to us of how gossip spreads, and the damage cannot be stopped by just an "I'm sorry."

Evenings on the mountain were always an adventure. Many times, we were able to take advantage of joining the conference that was currently in session and being challenged by excellent speakers. Other times, we would play board games or tell stories under the Coleman lantern. However, usually, it was "early to bed, early to rise"! We would be so tired from the day's activities that there would be little resistance from us, and we would willingly go out to our little nest in the back with our flashlights.

No matter what was needed in our lives, our parents made it a matter of prayer. They taught us what real faith was: that God would meet our needs and that He always answered our prayers. Although His answer might come as you must "wait a while" or even "No." A wonderful reminder of God's faithfulness was an often retold story about Papa's rescue when he was a small child. His primary family had journeyed many miles back to Missouri for a family reunion with all the paternal relatives. To take advantage of the bounty in the woods, many of the uncles were dispersed to pick nuts and berries, while others cut wood in anticipation of the early winter. Papa, as youngest of the four children in his family, was just four years old and went along with the fruit pickers. Grandma had dressed him in a bright-red hat and coat to keep warm on the journey. He was given a little bucket and instructed to fill it to the top. However, it soon began to thunder, and the sky lit up with lightning. He became very frightened and made a beeline for the house and the sanctuary of Grandma's apron.

As often is the case when there are many adults working on a project together, and no one is specifically assigned to watch a child, Papa's leaving was unobserved by the hard-working adults. Neither did anyone miss him for quite a while. Apparently, as he ran through the woods, he tried to climb over an old split log. As he climbed, it rolled, catching his body in a secure trap. Although he wiggled desperately, the more he struggled, the firmer he was caught. As the storm intensified, the temperature dropped, and it began to snow. The family members quickly left their chores and headed back to the warmth and protection of the farm. Suddenly, someone realized no one had the littlest child in his red hat and coat. Immediately, all the family and neighbors were mobilized to search.

Finally, in the darkness, someone noticed a red stain in the snow. They quickly checked it out and dug through the new fallen snow to find the little red cap on Papa's head. He was literally buried in the snow, although the branches had trapped some air for him to breathe. Upon the discovery, an uncle fired a gunshot into the air to alert other searchers that he had been found. They quickly wrapped him up in warm jackets and ran to the farmhouse. His grandfather put him in a tub of snow water and vigorously rubbed his hands and feet to restore circulation. They utilized a common medicinal remedy of the time: a stiff shot of whiskey to help warm his insides. Contrary to all medical expectations, he did not even lose any fingers or toes. He did not develop pneumonia and appeared none the worse for his experience. The relieved family all agreed that day that God had something very special for that little boy to do, since his life had been so miraculously spared.

His own child would experience a similar "lost" situation during the next generation! The Blue Bird troop (initial phase of Camp Fire Girls) went on a field trip to the large Griffith Park in Los Angeles. Although it was probably a birthday party for the troop leader's daughter, the purpose was not stored in our memory banks. All the children were having a wonderful time on the playground. They were all scattered around the equipment and running back and forth. My favorite thing was the old wooden push merry-go-round. I would never tire of running as fast as possible while pushing the bar and then jumping onto the wooden flooring as it spun around. Holding on tightly as the centrifugal force pushed against our little bodies, all would scream in delight. In the excitement, I never realized the composition of the children on the merry-go-round had changed; there was not one Blue Bird vest in sight.

Apparently, one of the adults realized time had slipped by, and it was way past the designated time to leave the park to meet the parents. In the chaos of loading up in the parking lot, there was a miscount of Blue Birds. The cars all took off, leaving me contently pushing the merry-go-round. All at once, I realized that no one was playing with me that looked familiar, and the playground seemed increasingly quiet. I did not see any friendly faces or kids with Blue Bird vests on. An icy cold fear initially surged through me as I ran back to the picnic tables. They were all empty! There were no cars in the parking lot, and the sun was going down. I had been left behind.

It did not occur to me to just sit and cry. I just knew that I had better get moving so I would get home before my parents got worried. I was fairly familiar with the way home because we passed Griffith Park every time we went to church at Lake Street Baptist. So I started trudging down the boulevard. It seemed much longer to reach the big fountain on the corner than it did when we were in the car. Little flower shops, familiar stores, and restaurants that we usually buzzed by in the car seemed to take forever to put behind me. I just kept putting one foot in front of the other, saying the family motto: "I think I can, I think I can!" I was curiously not afraid, for I felt confident that God had sent His guardian angel to be with me on the journey. No one on the street seemed to think it odd that a little girl was hurrying down the sidewalk alone at that time of evening.

It seemed to me that the greater fear I had was causing my parents to be disappointed in my lack of responsibility to the instructions of the group leader than I was afraid of the long walk. After walking several miles and watching the sun sink down on the horizon, I lost faith that I would reach home before dinner. Instead, my anxiety increased about missing the turns in the gathering darkness. A familiar verse we had learned in Sunday school echoed in my head, "Be anxious for nothing." The verse reminded me to have more faith. Suddenly, I heard a screech of tires and a familiar bass voice yelling, "There she is." Papa ran up and scooped me into his strong arms. At that time, I could not understand his relief and tears of thankfulness at finding his lost child. I did not really feel lost, just left. I was only in the wrong place, but I knew where I was all the time.

It was not until I also became a parent and temporarily lost one of my own children that I experienced that body-draining fear and the need to fervently pray for God's intervention and help while searching for that child. I then understood a little of what my parents felt as the Blue Birds got back to the neighborhood, and the adults realized one was missing. A search party was quickly organized, and most of the parents went back to the park to search. However, my parents knew their child and the faith they had nurtured in God's leading, so Papa's search began on the route back home. It was amazing to all those who gathered that I was not crying or afraid. I felt confident it was just a matter of time until my parents found me, or I made it all the way back home. My Papa might not know where I was for the time being, but we both understood that the heavenly Father knew exactly where I was at all times, understood all of our fears, and was watching out for me each minute of that long journey.

At the Corning First Baptist church, Papa's last full-time pastorate, all the extended family had come up for Christmas. All the grandkids had a great time playing in the big three-level house on five acres filled with all kinds of animals. Papa had an old donkey that they could all ride, goats to watch and even learn to milk, calves to herd, indoor and outdoor cats, and even a porcupine, although Papa was the only one that could hold him without threat from his spines.

Papa was never too tires or busy to play with his grandkids.
Here he is giving little Mikie a flying ride

Mama demonstrated how easy riding the donkey could be

Papa loved the country churches for then he could expand
his menagerie. He raised a drop calf on a very small mother
goat who willingly got up on the milkstand to let the calf
nurse, soon he was bigger than she was but still eating

Papa could hold his special pet porcupine with never a fear
of getting hit by sharp quills. No one else ventured close
to his special pet whose name was Porky of course

Papa had finally given in to Mama's pleas for a swimming pool for her to cool off on those very hot summer
days after she taught all day at school. The huge ten-foot
deep end hole was dug in the backyard just before our family's Christmas visit. Our son, Theron (their first grandson),
was just three years old, but we already knew he was prone
to sleepwalking, especially in a different environment. After
a huge meal, lots of games, and catching up conversation,
everyone headed to bed. Our family was down in the rum-
pus room of the basement in sleeping bags. As mothers will
do, I wakened in the night, suddenly terrified something
was very wrong. I quickly checked the kids and found there
was no one in Theron's little sleeping bag. A quick check
of the bathroom and the whole downstairs found no child.
There was no child found in the entire house. My imagi-
nation flew to every terrible scenario as I woke the entire
household to start the search. In my mind, I was afraid we
would find his little body smashed at the bottom of the
pool hole. Papa and my husband Don started searching the

outside foot by foot. They went together in concentric circles around the house, not leaving any section unscanned. The rest of us checked every other possible hiding place in the house and garage. All our voices echoed in the night, "Theron, Theron, where are you baby?" Finally, all the searchers heard a little scream from the bottom of the acreage where the creek ran through the property. Papa and Don found Theron standing in the cold water up to his ankles, terrified in the dark and feeling all alone (except for his guardian angel, all agreed). Somehow, in God's providence, the little guy had navigated past all the obstacles, including the pool hole, rock walls, gardens, etc. and awakened as the cold water covered his little feet. We all stood in the dark, thanking God for His faithful protection and the answer to our fervent prayers.

At Christmas the grandkids were always delighted
to see "Mommy kissing Santa Claus."

Another incident happened a few years later at the Christmas gathering (now there were four grandchildren to watch). However, as commonly happens in shared responsibility for children, with many adults contributing their stories and little bodies running everywhere, no one was actually watching the little ones' activities. The kids had been sledding down the staircase on old cardboard boxes, and somehow, one found a one-thousand pill bottle of Flintstone Vitamins in Linda's suitcase. They all knew they tasted great like candy, and this was their chance to get big bites. All four kids started rapidly eating. Linda went downstairs to check on the quiet kids (always a scary sign) and screamed, "Help! All the kids are eating Flintstone vitamins!" Thankfully, their Uncle Dan was a physician in the next town, and a quick call gave us simple but effective instructions to prevent severe consequences. All the kids continued to proclaim their innocence (even with the colored stains on their lips and fingers). My Don ran to the local drugstore to obtain Epicac, a very effective emetic. We lined the kids up next to the bathtub, gave them all the dosage required, and waited for the inevitable results. Hundreds of pills shot out of their mouths in the resulting huge emesis. The youngest granddaughter had even swallowed the dehumidifying capsule, which could have had very serious results. Even with the evidence in front of them, they all proclaimed innocence, "I didn't do it!"

4 grandkids enjoying a human sled down
the staircase of Corning home

Papa and Mama had built their dream house on that acreage and enjoyed every minute of the construction process and all the activities on the acre. One day, while Papa was at church working, and Mama was teaching at the local school, the sound of fire engines rent the air, and smoke was rising from their hill. The firefighters quickly extinguished the flames and found the origin was the large aquarium Papa had built in the wall of the stairwell. Apparently, a wire had shorted and caught the surrounding wood on fire. Although he lost all his fish and their aquarium and many of the cherished books in his study, most of the house was saved. The insurance company covered all the repairs including smoke damage, but some things were irreplaceable. As a sign of God's faithfulness, a large plaque Mama had made in ceramics class was preserved, "God so loved the world that He gave His only Son…"

Building the Corning House, Papa even let his first
grandson, Theron Wade McDaniel help nail the studs

Papa even used him as a helper with
chores like driving the tractor

Through all these life experiences, we found that no matter the circumstances, mountaintop or valleys, that we journeyed through, we knew God's faithfulness was there to bring us through and restore us.

Chapter 8

THE FRUIT OF THE SPIRIT IS LOVE, JOY, PEACE, PATIENCE, KINDNESS, GOODNESS, FAITHFULNESS...
GENTLENESS

Reading the stories of Jesus's life was where we learned what gentleness really meant. His tenderness in dealing with people became the goal we aspired to obtain. However, our earthly parents were the closest example of gentleness that we actually observed. As most active children with vivid imaginations, our subconscious sometimes came up with terrible nightmares in the darkest of the night. We would fly out of our beds, screaming bloody murder, and searching for the comfort and protection that only the arms of our parents would bring. We would crawl into their bed under the down comforter and know we were safe in their arms. They never would send us back to bed with a scolding but would tuck us next to them with soothing words. They never complained about cold feet or a bony elbow interfering with their own rest. Somehow, the next morning, we would wake up in our own beds, with only dim memories of the distressing night problems. One night, I dreamed that all the fish in Papa's tank had jumped out and were all over the floor. I was afraid to put my feet over the edge of the bed, for I did not want to squish their little bodies. Papa got up and carried me to the bathroom so he could turn on the lights and prove it was just a dream. No matter how small the problem may have seemed to them, if it was a worry for us, they were there to listen. Very seldom did they ever have to give advice. It was usually enough for us to talk it through, and the answer would become usually very clear.

Any little physical hurt, scrape, or cut was immediately cared for with lots of TLC (tender loving care) and the magic red solution kept in the medicine cabinet called Merthiolate. If it was a scary big wound, the "big gun"—iodine—, was utilized. Even though the cleansing and treatment stung and sometimes caused big tears, we knew that the treatment was to keep us from getting sick or the wound infected. A parent's gentle kiss to make the "owie" better usually did just that, and we would run back to our activities. Even later in our teen years, when it was not usually physical pain but the emotional trauma of broken relationships or conflicts, the gentle spirits of our parents listening empathetically to the problem did much to restore us to an even keel. Somehow, they were able to make even broken hearts mend.

One of the best examples of physical gentleness occurred when we would bring in a hurt finger or toe inflicted with a painful splinter or a rose thorn. Papa was a super specialist at getting these out with minimal, if any, discomfort. He used distraction, alternate stimulus, such as pinching the part below the wound, and verbal reinforcement of his specialized procedure skills to make each incident bearable. Before we knew it, the splinter or thorn would be on the table as a trophy to display for our courage and Papa's proficiency as a gentle "splinter surgeon."

Probably the best way we learned about gentleness in our relationships was observing how our parents treated each other. Rarely did we hear their voices raised in argument, but there was always underlying encouragement and support in all circumstances. They were quick to verbally reassure each other that a project was well-done and appreciated. During Papa's first pastorate in Buttonwillow, Mama was plagued by migraine headaches for a period of time, usually on Sunday afternoons. Looking back on it from a medical perspective now, I am sure that the additional stresses of learning all the responsibilities the congregation had for a pastor's wife certainly contributed. She wore so many hats; no wonder her head hurt. After a quick lunch, Papa would put her to bed with the drapes closed and a wet cloth on her head. He would offer the cure-all aspirin and tell her to try and sleep. He would then entertain us kids with outdoor games or projects while she rested quietly. They were a real team! Yet we observed the biblical principle of submission demonstrated as Papa assumed his God-given leadership role in the household. All major decisions were gently made by him, with much input from Mama. He had quickly learned to depend on her wisdom and sense of perspective in all situations.

We girls understood that Mama had a wonderful way of making him think whatever she wanted was his own idea from the start. Maybe today, some would call that behavior manipulation, but we thought it was brilliant tactic. She was truly a master at getting her ideas and projects started. Whether it was a new rock garden (essential in all their homes), a fishpond and waterfall, or a baby lamb that needed to be adopted, somehow, regardless of initial protests or lack of resources, time, or energy, Papa would be seen with the shovel, making the first holes for the latest project. It was interesting to see him utilize that same strategy with stubborn church board members. He would plant the seed of a great idea or solution to a problem and let it simmer and grow until they thought it was their own idea and jumped on board.

The little country church had an acre of grass around it that could be useful if developed into a play area to help keep the kids occupied. In a four-block town, there was little recreation available, so it was easy for kids to get in trouble after school. Papa thought he could make a miniature golf course where the kids could play, as well as a volleyball and badminton court. There was much discussion about how that would interfere with the landscaping and quiet dignity of the church. Soon, however, Papa had the miniature golf course put in with all donated supplies and, mostly, his hard work. The church yard became a gathering place for all the town children as they learned to play together.

Often, Mama became the mediator when there was a misunderstanding or conflict in the church family. She was a great listener and could soothe even the most ruffled feathers. We found it very interesting that church families can disagree about almost anything. Sometimes, business meetings go out of control and become shouting matches as everyone tries to have their own way over something. We had heard about churches that split over the color of the carpet, type of hymnal, or who was to be the next person to join the Board. What would Jesus say if He heard such petty things caused conflict in His church? Our parents were zealous at keeping the peace and reminding people of the real purpose of God's church: to follow the example of the Prince of Peace who exemplified gentleness in all His dealings with His followers.

Chapter 9

THE FRUIT OF THE SPIRIT IS LOVE, JOY, PEACE, PATIENCE, KINDNESS GOODNESS, FAITHFULNESS, GENTLENESS, AND...

SELF-CONTROL

In each of our parents' ministry assignments, as PKs (preacher's kids), we were held to the highest standard of behavior. It was very important to our parents that we reflect a good example for the other kids in the congregation. We began to understand the importance of "self-control"

under our parents' gentle but persistent and consistent pattern of expectation and discipline. They were firm believers in the proverb, "Spare the rod, and spoil the child." What we were supposed to do and not to do in every occasion was clearly stated. These standards were expectations that were kept with great consistency. When we deviated from the "straight and narrow," we knew retribution was coming quickly and fairly. Usually, Mama would give a swift spank or withhold a valued privilege. Papa though, as we got older, had us climb our favorite tree, select a nice switch, climb down and tell him exactly our understanding of the transgression. He would say, "What did Nancy do? You know Papa loves you, but your legs need to remember not to ride your bike in the alley, play ball in the street, etc." At our desperate yells of "I'm sorry!" he would reply, "Yes, but are you sorry enough not to do it again?"

To help us remember the importance of obedience, one of our earliest memorized parts of Scripture was Ephesians 6:1–2, "Children obey your parents in the Lord for this is the right thing to do." It was so meaningful that we were certain that our own boys learned these verses at an early age. As a reminder too, all of it was posted on the refrigerator door. We knew it was another way to say the answer to "why" rather than "because I said so."

Sometimes, Mama had the most difficulty with her hubby when playing with us got out of hand. Our big sister Judy remembers big trouble when she and Papa were watering the lawn, and a water fight resulted. Soon, everyone was soaked, and Papa came running through the house with the hose, trying to beat everyone to the backyard and have the last squirt. It was not difficult to imagine who was on the receiving end of Mama's discipline after that incident.

We girls were usually very compliant and really desired our parents to be proud of us, so disobedience was an unusual problem. Although our big sister learned the hard way that Papa still meant what he said when rules were laid down. Even when she was old enough to begin dating, she had a little difficulty getting in at the agreed curfew time. She received a stern warning and discussion of the rule the first couple of times, with a resulting promise that it would never happen again. One time, Papa decided she needed an object lesson to remember her promise, so he tied a little dead mouse by the tail on the pull chain of the back porch light. At the curfew hour, they shut off the lights and quietly went to bed. As Judy tried to sneak in the dark silent house undetected, she reached up to pull on the porch light. Her screams made certain that her arrival time was etched in everyone's memories, including the neighbors. Until her wedding day, she was never again late home without calling and getting an agreed extension.

Our parents had the most difficulty with me. I was the tomboy, never content to play house or sit at tea parties with dolls. I demanded action and adventure. Most times when they could not find me, they searched the treetops. One of my favorite refuges was a comfortable fork in the tree branches where I could lose myself with a special adventure story. My impulsiveness and need for a challenge kept me in constant trouble. Even when we were very small and still wearing Dr. Denton pajamas with their snap-down bottoms, I learned a very hard lesson. In the winter, our source of heat was a large potbelly stove. We would huddle around it for warmth during our bedtime story and prayer time. I had a bad habit of turning my back to the stove and getting as close to the heat as possible. One night, that was too close, and my little seat was roasted. I learned the hard way that the comfort of heat could quickly turn to the pain of burns. From that time until we moved from that house, Papa would sing, "Nancy had a little lamb, she tied him to the heater, and every time he turned around, he burned his little seater!"

One of the scariest misadventures that I had was after we had been treated to the original theatre production of Peter Pan, starring Mary Martin at the Shreiner's Auditorium in Los Angeles. The audience was captivated by the challenge from Tinker Bell to the children that "you can fly if you only believe." She really won me over, and I could not wait to join the children soaring effortlessly through the sky. The next day, with all the neighborhood kids lined up in the front yard to cheer me on, I climbed up the plum tree which gave me access to our rooftop. Carefully, I scaled the slippery shingles to the very top and walked to the edge of the peak. It really looked like a long way down, and I almost lost my courage. However, I was confident that I could fly just like Peter Pan and the kids, if I really believed. All the neighborhood kids yelled "you can do it" as I leaped out into space. Something did not work as I had planned, and I saw the ground rushing up in response to Newton's law of gravity. I landed kerplunk right in the center of Papa's carefully pruned and trimmed privet hedge. I was covered with scratches and bruises but escaped serious injury. I crawled out of the hedge in total disbelief. What could have gone wrong? I did not have the faith that was required by Tinker Bell!

The switching that I got for exercising poor judgment and making a bad choice was not as hurtful as my new understanding that the Law of Gravity was absolute. Even fairies could not change God's established laws, except in storybooks. It was only when I was much older that I heard Grandpa's version of our Papa's adventurous flight. Apparently, a frequent game of the boys of the ranch in Escondido was to climb to the top of a huge tree, jump over to the barn roof, slide down, and fall into the hay-stack while playing tag. One afternoon, the big brothers were closing in on our Papa, so instead of sliding down the roof, he jumped from the rooftop (just a little shortcut). Somehow, he managed to catch the side of the haystack and did not break anything either, but all the boys got in trouble for that one. I think it made Papa a little more understanding of his wild daughter's unsuccessful flight.

Early on, we were taught to do our share of the family chores. One of our favorites was Saturday morning washing clothes. Our job was fishing out the socks from the rinse water and feeding them through the wringer, then catching them quickly before they fell back into the wash water. It was a big challenge for little fingers and took great concen-tration. We got pretty good at it, and Mama let it be our job without such close supervision. One Saturday, she went into the house to get the next load of dirty clothes while I finished the sock detail. For some reason, as I reached around the wringer to quickly catch the sock, I did not let go of the original end. My fingertips were caught with the sock in the wringer. In total disbelief, I watched the wringer gobble up my arm. My screams brought Mama running to the scene. She quickly crashed down on the wringer release before great damage was done, even though the wringer had gone all the way to my armpit.

Mama had been praying for some time for a new washing machine. The old wringer one was quite stretched out and not quite up to the task of getting extra water out. That day, she was thankful that it was not a tight new one. Somehow, again I had escaped broken bones or serious injury, even though my arm was battered and bruised as were my spirits. Papa, although grateful that the washer was old and no longer as tight, wondered out loud how my guardian angel would survive until I grew up.

Another wild weekend afternoon, the neighborhood kids decided to play a game of baseball in the street. (That was an established big NO in our household.) However, they needed a catcher, and our parents were taking a much-needed nap, so the coast was clear. I quickly joined the game. Things went well for some time until an enthusiastic batter swung back with a mighty swish, connecting to my head instead of the little baseball. Frightened children scrambled for help as I lay in the street. I was left with a giant goose egg and a big headache, plus the knowledge that a blow a little further down my temple could have killed me. The dangers of street baseball that day became a lot more than cars driving down the lane.

I never enjoyed playing with fancy dolls like my sister, who had a bunch of storybook dolls, but I did have a favorite companion doll, Susie Q. With her painted wooden head and soft cloth body, she was wonderful for dragging all over on my adventures. As my interest in health and illness began to grow, I determined that Susie Q was in great distress and probably needed an appendectomy, like my little sister had just endured. While my parents were doing parent-type responsibilities, I carefully collected the necessary equipment. Little nail scissors were perfect for the abdominal incision. As I causctiously snipped through the cloth, sure enough, I found a knot of cotton in her tummy. That was carefully incised, and the wound thoroughly irrigated by the entire bottle of merthiolate. A few careful stitches and a dressing made from a diaper completed the procedure. Imagine the trouble I was in when the red merthiolate started dripping all over from the cloth skin. Much to my dismay, I found that rather than being thrilled that I had saved the doll from the severe complications of appendicitis, my parents were very upset with the operation results, especially all the red stains on the furniture and floor.

Schoolwork was never a problem for us. We always accepted it as a wonderful challenge. Our parents expected us to only do our best (which they interpreted as As). If our report card had something less, a careful discussion ensued, with a plan formulated to make necessary improvements before the next card came. Papa was always proud of our schoolwork and reminded us often in a joking way that he had also been an outstanding student (usually outstanding in the hall). He told us frequently about how little boys viewed school as an opportunity to scare teachers with frogs in their desks, etc. His most upsetting misadventure at school was when all of the kids in the class had a big dislike for the new teacher and elected Papa to scare her. On the way to school, he caught a garden snake to use for his planned mischief. He tucked it into his shirt to get it into the classroom, and when he found the teacher had stepped out for a moment, he slipped the snake into her top drawer where the class roll was kept. When she opened the drawer and saw the snake, she screamed and ran upstairs for the principal. While she was gone, Papa captured the little snake and tossed it out the window. The poor teacher was left humiliated when the principal could find no snake to substantiate her story. He determined she was imagining the whole thing. Not one classmate ever squealed on Papa as they all enjoyed the discomfort of their least favorite teacher. Fortunately for him, he grew up to develop a great respect for teachers. This respect was indeed fortunate since his wife, daughter, and grandsons all pursued that profession.

During his ministry at West Hollywood, Papa returned to his passion of playing chess. Anytime that he could find an opponent, and he had a little time, out came the chessboard. He found himself thinking of better moves and strategies all through the day. Finally, when he found himself mentally moving members of the congregation like chess pieces as he formulated better strategies for winning, he realized the game had gone too far. That was the last time we saw him play chess, although he enjoyed all other board games. He also got over his father's prohibition of playing cards. The only card game we could play when we were little was Old Maid.

Christmas at West Hollywood with Teenie and Bongo

We came to appreciate a type of "Whit wisdom." If we had difficulty with public speaking, Papa would reassure us that it was genetic. He claimed that when he was a young lad, Grandpa had made him a substitute usher at church when a regular usher called in sick. Grandpa gave him many instructions, including the first row was reserved for the choir, and no one else could sit there. He repeated it several times to be sure the instructions were clear. While Papa was busy talking, a large matronly woman firmly planted herself in the middle of the front row. Papa was sent down to ask her to move to another seat. Each footstep forward increased his apprehension. He was terrified and could not look at her in the eye as he said (reportedly): "Marden me, padam, you are occupuing the wrong pie, may I sew you to another sheet or would you prefer a chew in the back of the perch."

Papa also claimed that he had a summer job selling concessions at the baseball game. All he had to learn was the product names available to shout to potential customers. His first time out with the rack of peanuts, popcorn, chewing gum, and soda almost ended in disaster as he yelled, "Get your peacorn, popnuts, sodagum, and chewingwater here." Papa really enjoyed getting his "tangue tonguled," but it kept us in stitches and never got old.

It became even more difficult for our literary memories when he mutilated the little poem, Twinkle Twinkle Little Star. His version still resounds in my mind every time I look at the Heavens and see the beautiful stars. Papa claims that when a drunk looked up to the stars he quoted, "Starkle, starkle, little twink. Who the heck you are I think. I'm not under the alcofluence of inchohol like some thinkle peep I are. I fool so feelish I don't know who is me and the drunker I long here, the sitter I be."

He would also challenge anyone to use these words in one sentence—defeat, defense, and detail. These were a very difficult combination to meld together, but Papa did it easily—"Defeat went over defense, before detail." He could never resist the urge to share these WHITACISMS with any bunch of kids. He loved to play on words. Spelling was always a game and a challenge but would become very difficult when Papa started in. He would ask, "How do you pronounce To?" The reply was always to. How do you pronounce *TOO*? Of course, too. How do you pronounce two? That is another two. Then what is the second day of the week? If you were not very careful, it is almost impossible not to say Tuesday after your brain is into twos.

Even though Mama usually was responsible for making sure we had our work done for school, Papa sometimes got involved when he felt intervention was necessary between the teachers and us. When we arrived in the little town of Buttonwillow, we were both younger than the other children in our classes, most of whom were migrant children with little educational consistency. Papa took on the whole faculty and then the school board when they suggested my little sister go back a year for socialization purposes, even though she had completed the year's goals exceptionally well. Another time he intervened was when I was a senior in high school, and he found me carefully copying a chapter from a geography book. When he asked why I was doing this time-consuming mindless task, he found out this had been an assigned punishment for the whole class due to a few people misbehaving. Sure enough, the next morning, he was in the principal's office investigating the value of this type of assignment. The whole class cheered when the teacher said the assignment was no longer required.

Self-control may have been hardest when dealing with our ice cream addiction. Papa loved all types, but chocolate was supreme. Mama and I loved pineapple coconut although it was really hard to find. In Hanford church, they were given a chest freezer. Papa became good friends with the owner of Superior Dairy. He trusted Papa so much he gave him a key to the building and the giant freezer, so he could refill his stash whenever it got low. He would eat ice cream with a scoop of peanut butter for a snack. It would be probable to think he was big as a barn, but he always ran it off. Mama attempted to teach us excellent table manners so we would fit in with all social experiences. We would know which fork to use and how to pass food properly. Papa would undo her efforts by saying things in response to a hostess suggesting seconds: "My sufficiency is sufficed! Anymore would be obnoxious to my capacity"! She reminded us often that a simple "No, thank you" is much more elegant.

The principles of self-control and discipline that we grew up with brought us through the difficult standards required by the institutions of higher learning later encountered in our pursuits of our chosen professions. However, one of the lessons that we never learned but sorely needed was how to say no to requests for help. This omission caused us to later become overcommitted and strung out at times, with both work and church obligations. Even later, after classes and book reads on prioritizing, that elusive word NO was difficult for us to use in our daily lives.

Although, sometimes, we may have felt that we were missing some of the special trappings in life, such as fancy clothes, more than two pairs of shoes (one for play, and one for church), television, or new cars, we realized that what our family shared in love, joy, and peace were worth far more than any material things. Our childhood was filled with a treasure chest of memories, and we found we were using many of our parents' techniques in raising our own children. Many times, as we faced difficult decisions or problems in our adult lives, we realized that cloaking them with love, patience, and kindness would usually bring positive outcomes.

Our prayer continues to be that others will see the "fruit of the Spirit" reflected in our own lives as we surely saw them displayed in our wonderfully loving parents' lives. They were a wonderful example until their dying breaths. Papa was an example of all these attributes as he fought the horrors of bone cancer. Mama's last prayer request to our pastor was "Pray that God takes me home before I wear out my girls." Although she lived for several more days, those were the last words she spoke.

Our parents and their contributions to our lives will always remain in our hearts! Their example will be what we strive to keep in our own lives as long as we continue on this earth, and our prayer is that those examples will go down to our children and grandchildren. They left us with a true legacy of the Fruit of the Spirit: *love, joy, peace, patience, kindness, goodness, faithfulness, gentleness,* and *self-control.*

AFTERWORD

It is important to note that this account of our lives may be slightly altered from facts as others knew them. All of this came from my own recollection and is seen through my bias. Since I began writing this epistle, our Papa lost his battle with metastatic cancer, and the Lord called him home to Heaven at the age of eighty-five. The bulletin of his memorial service gives his girls final memories of their wonderful Papa (enclosed). Our dear Mama managed to be salt and light for one year still in their little home in Hemet. We then moved her up to Northern California so we could help with doctor's visits and other needs. Although none of us even believed she would live long without her fifty-nine-year love of her life, she surprised everyone by being a witness of faith and God's love for the next seven years. We told her goodbye just a few weeks after her eighty-fifth birthday. We are confident that they had an amazing reunion in Heaven and definitely heard from their Lord Jesus, "Well done thou good and faithful servants."

SPECIAL THANKS to my friends Stan and Sharon Smith for reading through the fourth rewrite of this manuscript and making valuable suggestions and identifying most of the errors in spelling and punctuation. Extra thanks for Sharon's patience spending hours trying to teach a technologically challenged person to efficiently use a new laptop computer.

MORE THANKS to my granddaughters: Shannon McDaniel for the wonderful cartoon illustrations at the chapter beginnings and for the drawing of our parents on the following page. Also thanks to Samantha McDaniel for creative direction and encouragement to get the project done.

And to my beloved husband of fifty-eight years, Don McDaniel, for his patience and understanding during the very long process of multiple revisions needed to get all these memories in an acceptable form.

CELEBRATING
THE LIFE OF
J. Leland Whitaker
December 2, 1913 - March 7, 1999

MEMORIAL SERVICE

DAUGHTERS REMEMBER PAPA
"WALKING THE TALK"

From our earliest memories our Papa modelled the "fruit of the Spirit" as he patiently taught us basic Christian principles.

LOVE: Our concept of God the Father's love for us was easy to accept as we observed our Papa's loving care. We saw how tenderly a man loves his wife & how cherished Mama felt. Our hope was God would bring a Godly man to love us as Papa loved Mama.

JOY: Our home was full of laughter and fun regardless of the circumstances. Papa made all of life a true adventure.

PEACE: We were always securely kept from outward turmoil and tenderly protected from the onslaught of evil in the world.

PATIENCE: We all learned this hard lesson together through God's plan of trials.

GENTLENESS: From taking out splinters painlessly, comforting loss from broken relationships, putting up with the crisis of teen girls, or listening to crushed dreams and plans—Papa was so gentle.

GOODNESS: Our home was always open to anyone night or day. He delighted in encouraging friends and was available any time to help when needed.

MEEKNESS: He demonstrated controlled strength in many of life's difficult situations.

FAITH: By his example we learned to trust and obey walking by faith not by sight.

SELF CONTROL: Except with coffee or ice cream!

Celebrating
85 Years of Giving
Eva A. Whitaker

November 9, 1921 – December 20, 2006

I am standing upon the seashore. A ship at my side spreads her white sails to the morning breeze and starts for the blue ocean. She is an object of beauty and strength. I stand and watch her until at length she hangs like a speck of white cloud just where the sea and sky come to mingle with each other.

Then someone at my side says: "There, she is gone!"

"Gone where'!"

Gone from my sight. That is all. She is just as large in mast and hull and spar as she was when she left my side and she is just as able to bear her load of living freight to her destined port.

Her diminished size is in me, not in her. And just at the moment when someone at my side says: "There, she is gone!" there are other eyes watching her coming, and other voices ready to take up the glad shout: "Here she comes!"

And that is dying.

Henry Van Dyke

We prayed for God to take Mama to Heaven away from the pain and suffering. When that prayer was answered, the great sense of loss was mixed with joy knowing God was welcoming her home. We will surely miss him until we are all together again. Our continued prayer is that what Mama walked &

talked will be reflected in each life that she touched as we all strive to "Keep Looking Up".

Thank You for sharing in this special day with us.

We Love You!

CHURCHES THEY SERVED

EASTMONT METHODIST CHURCH
Papa was music director
  1935–1939
Mama's home church
  1928–1937
Where their wedding reception was held in 1939

SALINAS COMMUNITY
First full time church
Assistant pastor
  1939-1941
TRINITY METHODIST
Youth Director
  1941-1943

first Presbyterian Church

555 E Street

SAN BERNARDINO, CALIFORNIA

Phone 394-77

STANLEY FREDERICK GEORGE...Pastor
        1190 College Drive — Phone 385-20

LELAND WHITAKER............Director of Music and Christian Education
        998 D Street — Phone 442-67

MISS DORIS J. SISCHO, Organist   MRS. W. N. VAUGHAN, Asst. Organist

CHARLES KELLAM...Caretaker

We welcome all to the worship of God and the fellowship of His people
in the name of Jesus Christ our Lord.

HOLLYWOOD FIRST BAPTIST CHURCH

Las Palmas and Selma - Telephone HI 7343

HAROLD L. PROPPE, M.A., B.D., Ph.D.
Minister

J. Leland Whitaker
Director of Christian Education

Everett L. Anderson   Ruth Willey Anderson
Director of Music   Organist

OUR MISSIONARY INTERESTS
Mr. and Mrs. Paul Uhlinger, Belgian Congo; Dr. and Mrs. A. G. Boggs, India

"The Friendly Colonial Church in the Heart of Hollywood"

LAKE STREET BAPTIST
1949–1952

BUTTONWILLOW
1952–1954

1954 -1957

WEST HOLLYWOOD
BAPTIST CHURCH

*Cordially Invites
You To Attend
Its Services*

J. Leland Whitaker
Pastor

Sunday School ....9:45 A. M.
Morning Worship ....11:00 A. M.
Youth Groups ....6:30 P. M.
Evening Service ....7:30 P. M.
Wed., Prayer, Bible Study ....7:30 P. M.

8252 Melrose Avenue, Los Angeles
Phone: WE 7002

LAKESIDE COMMUNITY CHURCH 1958–1962

139

CORNING FIRST BAPTIST CHURCH

1967–1981

The Congregation of the First Baptist church of Corning has built a beautiful new sanctuary and Sunday School unit. Their old building was built in 1903, so the new building has been needed for a long time. Services were first held in the new building on August 11, 1968. The Sunday School unit has classrooms to care for 200, a large fireside room is used as a youth center as well as a fellowship hall.

The Sanctuary has a very high roof line which makes it look like a church building. Padded pews seating 250 make for comfort and the red carpet add beauty to the interior. The church has a membership of 246 with over 200 average morning attendance. The evening service ranges between 60 and 90 in attendance.

Although the church is beautiful the most important part of the church is the christian fellowship and the working together of the members. There is a common interest in the proclaiming of the Gospel of God's love thru Christ. The three youth groups with their sponsors and the missionary Society with its three circles working on mission "White Cross" orders and the whole churches interest in missions show the work and interest of the church. One of the main emphases of the church is sponsoring Evangelical christian messages. The Pastor is a Bible Preacher making the scripture a part of daily living for very person.

We believe that the Christian message is the answer for the problems of our society. There are so many who try to proclaim that the churches message is race, labor, equality for all. We contend that if the church fulfills its message of presenting the Saviour as the answer to man's need. Civil rights is not the message of the church. In Romans 1:14 we read "I am debtor both to the Greeks, and the Barbarians; both to the wise and to the unwise." The Christian is debtor to all men; debtor to bring and share what God has done for him with others. We do not find the Jesus of Bethlehem complaining of being born in the stable. We do not read of him seeking his rights as He is tried in the Judgment hall. He does not even complain because he hasn't a place to lay His head. He asks the Father to forgive those who put Him on the cross. This should be a guide for us today.

We believe that the christian message is the message of God's love for and to man. The church is in the wrong business when it assumes the role of wage control, housing control, picketing, and all other non-violent actions. The churches business is to proclaim the Love of God for men who are buried in the problems and sin of life. If a man is right in the heart he will be right toward all men. We cannot legislate love or kindness but we earn this privilege by being lovable and kind. The church must learn that the only message it has is a message lived thru the lives of the members. The pronouncements are meaningless unless those who read them read them from the lives of its people. The Christian message is "God so loved the world that He gave His only begotten Son." This Son was given not to reform governments, society, or social justices, but to redeem a lost people from their sins. God's Gift was to "whosoever will, let him come and take of the 'Water of Life' freely." If all individuals have the Love of God in their hearts then the whole of society will be changed.

> J. Leland Whitaker, pastor
> First Baptist Church
> Corning, California

One of Papa's many trips to the Holy Land this time he took Mama
and Linda & Husband Paul as well as 25 church members

HUME LAKE MEMORIES

Mama in our old station wagon in front of Hume Lake

Papa in front of the "almost" completed cabin

Nancy, Sharon Warkentine, and Linda on the trail at
Hume—this picture was turned into a postcard until
Hume no longer could afford to keep horses

Papa and Don McDaniel painting the cabin and each other.
Mama wanted it green so it blended with the tress

All 4 grandchildren on the trunk of the car in
the snow at Hume for Thanksgiving

Nancy & Linda remembering our parents after our traditional
hike around the lake picking up trash on the trail

DO PASTORS/MINISTERS REALLY RETIRE?

Papa retired from Corning First Baptist. His love for red socks prompted one of his parishioners to make a tie and special sock boutonniere for his retirement celebration

Papa and Mama in front of their retirement home on
five acres in Kelso WA on a hill overlooking I-5

Papa's retirement ministry included being Chaplain at Campus
Towers his church run retirement home that housed over 100

He had vesper services every Sunday afternoon,
frequent concerts during the week, and of course
checked on anyone who was ill or hospitalized

Their Kelso home was an inspiration to weary travelers on
I 5 reminding them of Jesus gift of life
1987

They celebrated
the 50th anniversary
June 11, 1989 at
the Kelso church

We gave a family
concert at the
Campus Towers
July 22, 1996. Papa
was no longer able
to stand for them
but still has his
powerful bass voice

Papa was always "cutting up" we loved every antic

Papa in the last stages of bone cancer still entertained us with his antics. He found on old wig and met his visitors.—Life was very difficult and he was ready to go to his Heavenly home

ABOUT THE AUTHOR

Nancy McDaniel has been married fifty-eight years to her husband, Captain Don, a UAL pilot for thirty of those years. They had two sons who wisely chose exceptional daughters-in-law and produced four grandchildren. The McDaniel family has lived on an acre in a small farm town in Northern California for forty-seven years. Nancy is a private pilot, with over 500 hours logged. She is also first mate on their Catalina 30 sailboat that sails up and down the SF Delta. She worked her entire career as an RN in public health, OB, and education. She loved teaching the community childbirth classes, Lamaze, and CPR as well as continuing education for the local hospital's nursing staff. She finally got her MPHA from USF and finished her work time teaching first year nursing students in the local college. She is very active in her church, serving in many ministry areas and attempting to practice what her parents preached about the Fruit of the Spirit.

CPSIA information can be obtained
at www.ICGtesting.com
Printed in the USA
LVHW091948310321
682892LV00034B/553